Calendar No. 193

| 112TH CONGRESS | SENATE | REPORT |
| 1st Session | | 112–96 |

TRAFFICKING VICTIMS PROTECTION REAUTHORIZATION ACT OF 2011

NOVEMBER 17, 2011.—Ordered to be printed

Mr. LEAHY, from the Committee on the Judiciary,
submitted the following

R E P O R T

together with

ADDITIONAL AND MINORITY VIEWS

[To accompany S. 1301]

[Including cost estimate of the Congressional Budget Office]

The Committee on the Judiciary, to which was referred the bill (S. 1301), to authorize appropriations for fiscal years 2012 through 2015 for the Trafficking Victims Protection Act of 2000, to enhance measures to combat trafficking in persons, and for other purposes, having considered the same, reports favorably thereon, with an amendment, and recommends that the bill, as amended, do pass.

CONTENTS

I. Background and Purpose of the Trafficking Victims Protection Reauthorization Act of 2011

Human trafficking is a modern-day form of slavery involving victims who are forced, defrauded, or coerced into labor or sexual exploitation. As documented in the State Department's annual Trafficking in Persons Report for 2011, millions of children, women, and men throughout the world continue to be trafficked every year, including thousands of victims who are present here in the United States. Traffickers use evolving methods of coercion—whether subtle or overt, physical or psychological—to force victims to work against their will.

In 2000, Congress passed the landmark, bipartisan Trafficking Victims Protection Act (TVPA), which provided law enforcement officials with tools to investigate and prosecute incidents of human trafficking, established severe criminal penalties for defendants convicted of trafficking crimes, enhanced services for human trafficking victims, and expanded prevention and education programs. Championed by the late Senator Paul Wellstone and Senator Sam Brownback, the original Trafficking Victims Protection Act drew upon the work and support of a broad coalition of advocacy organizations from across the political and social spectrum—groups dedicated to children's rights, human rights, and women's rights, as well as many religious organizations. Each subsequent reauthorization of the law—in 2003, 2005, and 2008—has been the product of bipartisan support in Congress.

The success of the original Trafficking Victims Protection Act, and its subsequent reauthorizations over the past decade, is evident not only by the number of criminal convictions secured against human traffickers but also by the number of States that have passed comprehensive anti-trafficking laws. According to a July 2011 study by the Polaris Project, 47 States and the District of Columbia have now passed human trafficking criminal laws.[1] Similarly, countries around the world have followed the lead of the United States and adopted laws and policies to combat human trafficking. Even with these successes, the Committee believes more can and should be done.

The Trafficking Victims Protection Reauthorization Act of 2011 reaffirms and augments the United States' commitment to fighting human trafficking. The bipartisan bill reported out of Committee expands enforcement tools and encourages interagency cooperation to identify victims, investigate offenses, and provide victim services. The bill also requires that this important work be done in a cost-effective way with maximum accountability and reporting to ensure that Federal money is being well spent. Despite the difficult cuts to authorization levels, which were made with recognition of the Federal Government's fiscal constraints, the reported bill maintains the core of the Trafficking Victims Protection Act while adding key provisions to strengthen and improve this law.

Among the most significant changes to the law are the creation of new tools and authorities that will enable the State Department to partner with the private sector and foreign governments, as well as promote partnerships between foreign governments and nongovernmental entities. These provisions of the bill were drafted in

---

[1] *See* http://www.polarisproject.org/what-we-do/policy-advocacy/state-policy/current-laws.

consultation with the Committee on Foreign Relations, and with the input of the Chairman, Senator Kerry of Massachusetts, and its Ranking Member Senator, Senator Lugar of Indiana.

Anti-trafficking efforts have historically focused on the three "P"s, which are prevention of the crime, prosecution of the perpetrators, and protection of the trafficked persons. Increased attention to a fourth "P," partnership, will better leverage available resources to end trafficking.

The legislation also expands the role that regional bureaus of the State Department will play in anti-trafficking efforts. Although the Office to Monitor and Combat Trafficking in Persons (G/TIP) is the Department's lead on anti-trafficking policies and programs, the regional bureaus are uniquely situated to help develop country-specific anti-trafficking strategies and goals with foreign government counterparts. Increased collaboration between regional bureaus and G/TIP, including the appointment of anti-trafficking officers in some U.S. embassies as authorized by the legislation, will improve communication with foreign government counterparts and strengthen diplomatic efforts around trafficking. Although the anti-trafficking officers will serve under Chief of Mission authority, the Committee expects that G/TIP will provide considerable input into their selection. The Committee also expects that the G/TIP office will direct, guide, and communicate with these officials regularly.

The bill also addresses trafficking crimes committed by diplomats serving in other countries, including the United States. Current law requires the Department of State, when compiling the Trafficking in Person Report, to consider "whether the government of the country vigorously investigates, prosecutes, convicts, and sentences public officials who participate in or facilitate severe forms of trafficking in persons." [2] While the plain meaning of the term "public official" includes diplomats representing the country abroad, the State Department has interpreted it more narrowly and has not included trafficking cases involving diplomats in previous reports. The bill corrects this confusion and explicitly requires reporting on trafficking by "diplomats and soldiers." [3] It is the Committee's expectation that action taken by foreign governments, and the United States Government, to respond to allegations of serious trafficking offenses committed by foreign diplomats and military personnel posted abroad will be included in the report in the future.

The bill also makes explicit that a government's failure to appropriately address public allegations against public officials, especially once such officials have returned to their home countries, shall be considered inaction under the criteria for determining whether the country is meeting minimum standards for eliminating trafficking. Finally, the Committee notes that the Secretary of State has not suspended the issuance of visas to non-citizens seeking to work for officials of a diplomatic mission or an international organization where there are credible allegations of abuse and state or institutional tolerance of those violations. Current law requires the Secretary to suspend these visa programs under such

---

[2] 22 U.S.C. § 7106(b)(7).
[3] The Committee intends the term "soldiers" to include all military personnel.

circumstances.[4] The Committee will monitor credible allegations of abuse and expects the Secretary to take actions as required by law.

Notably, the legislation reduces authorization levels for State Department programs, including for section 113(a) of the Trafficking Victims Protection Act of 2000,[5] which authorizes funds for G/TIP. These reductions are not intended to signal a shift in the Committee's priorities away from trafficking. Rather, they reflect the fact that the State Department receives anti-trafficking funds through the Foreign Assistance Act instead of through this specific authorization. In the decade since the TVPA's enactment in 2000, governments around the world have made great strides in combating trafficking. Much of that success may be attributed to the creation of G/TIP and the annual Trafficking in Persons Report. This Committee strongly supports the work of G/TIP and expects that it will continue to receive funding from the general State Department operating account at current or greater levels in order to fulfill its mandate.

Other significant changes include targeted increases in Federal funding for victim services provided by the Department of Justice, the Department of Health and Human Services, and their grantees. These services provide a lifeline to victims of trafficking who often have no other means to obtain housing, food, medical treatment, and counseling. In addition to meeting the direct needs of victims, these services are a central component in effective law enforcement efforts. As Principal Deputy Assistant Attorney General Mary Lou Leary emphasized in her testimony before the Committee, "victims who receive immediate physical, mental, and emotional support will be much more able and willing to participate in the investigation and prosecution of their traffickers."[6]

This increase in funding also reflects that much of the TVPA's success comes from a multidisciplinary response to human trafficking. That approach encourages close partnerships among victim service providers, State and local law enforcement, and Federal law enforcement, including the Federal Bureau of Investigation, U.S. Immigration and Customs Enforcement, U.S. Customs and Border Protection, U.S. Citizenship and Immigration Services, the Department of Labor, and Federal prosecutors. These partnerships leverage scarce resources and ensure a coordinated, multi-jurisdictional response. Although these agencies work closely together, the TVPA and its reauthorizations has also put into place structures to ensure that they do not duplicate each other's work. For example, the Senior Policy Operating Group (SPOG), established by statute in 2003, coordinates the work of multiple cabinet agencies to ensure that anti-trafficking efforts are synchronized and that projects avoid duplication.

The Office of Justice Programs (OJP) of the Department of Justice has also put in place additional accountability mechanisms to ensure that grant programs are effectively administered. Although the views offered by Senator Grassley and Senators Kyl, Sessions, Lee, and Coburn focus on a 2008 report by the Department of Jus-

---

[4] 8 U.S.C. § 1375c(a)(2).

[5] 22 U.S.C. § 7110(a).

[6] Testimony of Mary Lou Leary, "The Trafficking Victims Protection Reauthorization Act: Renewing the Commitment to Victims of Human Trafficking," before the Senate Comm. on the Judiciary, 112th Cong. (2011), available at http://judiciary.senate.gov/hearings/hearing.cfm?id=6344ca9cdcac94c57d1fa7ad3d740a6f.

tice Inspector General which criticized various aspect of grant management by OJP, they do not mention the Inspector General's subsequent 2011 report that praises OJP for making significant improvements in monitoring and oversight of grants. Most of those improvements have come with the establishment of the Office of Audit, Assessment, and Management (OAAM), which was created in 2005, but was not fully staffed until 2009. The Inspector General found that since OAAM began operating at capacity, OJP has "made significant improvements" and "developed a reasonable process for providing monitoring to a high volume of grants, which have allowed them to monitor grants totaling almost four times the award amount required by law."[7]

To ensure that funding is efficiently and effectively spent, the legislation also includes several accountability measures for programs administered by the Department of Justice. These provisions aim to ensure that grants are awarded to proper recipients, that funds are used as intended to benefit victims of trafficking, and that grants are properly supervised and administered. Among the accountability measures are annual audit requirements for a sample of grant recipients, with consequences for those recipients found to have problems that are not meaningfully addressed; a non-federal matching requirement for all grantees; restrictions on investments, tax status, and lobbying for grantees; and restrictions on administrative expenditures and conferences for the Department of Justice. These provisions were the product of detailed negotiations and careful consideration. They were specifically tailored to the needs and contours of the grant programs authorized under this Act and administered by the Department of Justice. They are intended to ensure that these particular grant programs work as intended, and to improve accountability, without excessively burdening grantees or preventing needed services from reaching victims.

As to accountability, Senators Kyl, Sessions, Lee, and Coburn assert that TVPA grants have been distributed based on faulty priorities and have been poorly managed. In fact, grants awarded pursuant to the TVPA have been effectively used to assist victims and to prevent, prosecute, and deter trafficking domestically and around the world. While the minority views assert that the State Department has not tracked with any precision large numbers of grants awarded, in fact the State Department has tracked those grants comprehensively by project, with grantees reporting on their work regularly. The State Department was only able to give partial responses in the one document cited by the minority views because that document contained responses to questions that called for grants to be classified in different ways than the ways the Department tracks them. The State Department has documented that 90 percent of projects funded by G/TIP included a victim protection component, 61 percent provided victim services, and 52 percent built the capacity of local law enforcement and prosecutors to go after traffickers.[8]

---

[7] U.S. Dep't of Justice, Office of the Inspector Gen., Semiannual Report to Congress, Oct. 1, 2010–March 31, 2011, at 58.
[8] G/TIP Response to Senator Tom Coburn's October 2011 Report, "Blind Faith: How Congress is Failing Trafficking Victims", November 2011, at 2–3.

Some awards are also criticized as duplicative when in fact they addressed related but distinct and separate needs.[9] The minority views, in criticizing spending on public awareness campaigns, also ignore the need for any comprehensive anti-trafficking strategy to include a prevention component, which includes public awareness, in addition to victim services, in order to reduce the number of victims going forward.

Nonetheless, it is important that grant programs, particularly those aimed at as important a problem as human trafficking, operate as effectively as possible. To this end, Chairman Leahy and Senator Grassley worked to address in the reported version of the bill the kinds of concerns expressed by Senators Kyl, Sessions, Lee, and Coburn. The reported bill contains new provisions to try to ensure that funds awarded under the TVPA translate to effective prevention, enforcement, and victim services successfully contributing to combating the scourge of human trafficking. The legislation as reported includes significant new accountability measures covering all TVPA grants administered by the Department of Justice. It focuses funding on the most important initiatives while eliminating or reducing funding for those that have been less successful in the past.

The reported bill focuses on domestic trafficking. Spending under the TVPA has been set up to ensure sufficient funding to make significant strides in dealing with domestic trafficking, while also acknowledging the need to address the massive scale of global trafficking and the fact that much domestic trafficking has roots in international trafficking rings. The Committee recognizes the need to ensure that domestic trafficking is sufficiently prioritized. For that reason, the reported bill adjusts authorization levels to increase the funds available for domestic trafficking victims relative to international victims.[10]

The bill improves cooperation between law enforcement agencies and victims. Current law allows the immediate family members of a trafficking victim in the United States to receive nonimmigrant status based on a fear of retaliation from the traffickers. Principal Deputy Assistant Attorney General Leary testified that this provision has proven helpful in stabilizing victims and encouraging them to participate in the criminal prosecution of their trafficker. "Our prosecutors have found that victims are better able to cooperate when their family members are out of the reach of the trafficker," she said.[11] The Department of Homeland Security shares

---

[9] Senators Kyl, Sessions, Lee, and Coburn cite grants to two organizations helping to combat trafficking in Chad. One of these grants, to Catholic Relief Services, focused on preventing trafficking of children in three high-risk communities. The second, distinct and complementary, grant to the International Organization for Migration focused on preventing trafficking at the macro level by improving government policy and the ability of non-governmental organizations to protect and provide services to victims. *See* G/TIP Response to Senator Coburn's Report, at 8. Similarly, two grants to the International Organization for Migration for a case management database were awarded because the initial grant proved very successful in leading to a tool that helped both with provision of services and with research to inform better policy choices. G/TIP awarded the second grant for expansion of the project. *Id.* at 8–9.

[10] The Committee also reaffirms, as the Department of Justice has already made clear, that TVPA funds can be used to provide services to domestic trafficking victims.

[11] Testimony of Mary Lou Leary, "The Trafficking Victims Protection Reauthorization Act: Renewing the Commitment to Victims of Human Trafficking," before the Senate Comm. on the Judiciary, 112th Cong. (2011), available at http://judiciary.senate.gov/hearings/hearing.cfm?id= 6344ca9cdcac94c57d1fa7ad3d740a6f.

this position and provided the following example at the Committee's hearing:

> In 2010, the Vermont Service Center successfully approved a mother of a sex trafficking survivor based on this new exception, and worked with the Department of State to facilitate her entry into the United States. The mother, who had received death threats by one of her daughter's traffickers, was able to reunite with her daughter and to testify at her daughter's trial." [12]

This legislation modestly augments the list of eligible relatives who may file as a derivative beneficiary of a "T" visa holder. Traffickers seek to control their victims by threatening not just immediate family members, but also grandchildren, step-children, nieces, and nephews. This authorization responds by allowing certain family members to apply to join the trafficking victim in the United States, but only if those family members face a present danger of retaliation in their home country by the traffickers. Family members who do not face retaliation would not be eligible under this modification.

The bill adds "fraud in foreign labor contracting," as defined by 18 U.S.C. § 1351, to the list of crimes for which victims may be eligible to apply for a "U" visa. Fraud in foreign labor contracting is difficult to prosecute because victims are often reluctant to come forward and report the crime for fear of being deported. Including this crime as a qualifying criminal activity for a "U" visa will encourage greater reporting, victim cooperation, and prosecution of this serious offense.

The bill also reduces authorization levels for investigations by U.S. Immigration and Customs Enforcement (ICE) of severe forms of trafficking in persons. This change is not intended to signal a desire to reduce ICE's role in fighting human trafficking. To the contrary, the Committee believes that ICE, and the Department of Homeland Security as a whole, play a critical role in identifying, investigating, and prosecuting human trafficking cases. That work is done through training with State and local law enforcement partners, victim assistance efforts, and the wide dissemination of information through public awareness campaigns in the United States and in foreign countries with high levels of trafficking. The reduction in authorized funding does not signal a shift in congressional priorities. Rather, it reflects the fact that ICE's anti-human trafficking efforts are funded by its annual appropriations, and not through this specific authorization.

This legislation also amends the information required to be included in the Attorney General's annual report regarding Federal agencies' efforts to implement anti-human trafficking measures. In particular, it adds a requirement to report on the effectiveness of various immigration protections for victims of human trafficking.

One of these immigration protections is Continued Presence (CP). This is a temporary, revocable immigration status provided to individuals identified by law enforcement as victims of human traf-

---

[12] Testimony of Kelly Ryan, "The Trafficking Victims Protection Reauthorization Act: Renewing the Commitment to Victims of Human Trafficking," before the Senate Comm. on the Judiciary, 112th Cong. (2011), available at http://judiciary.senate.gov/hearings/hearing.cfm?id= 6344ca9cdcac94c57d1fa7ad3d740a6f.

ficking. This status allows victims of human trafficking to remain in the United States temporarily during the ongoing investigation into the human trafficking-related crimes committed against them.

According to guidelines established by the Department of Homeland Security,[13] CP applications should be submitted immediately upon identification of a victim of human trafficking. A law enforcement officer can make this identification after receiving credible evidence that an alien is a victim of human trafficking. That evidence may consist of a credible victim statement alone.

Despite these widely circulated guidelines, the number of CP applications that have been granted has declined in recent years and is disproportionately small compared to the estimated number of human trafficking victims present in the United States. According to the 2011 State Department's Trafficking in Persons Report, only 186 individuals received Continued Presence in 2010. This was a significant drop from 2009, when 299 individuals received this temporary protection. This decline is troubling, especially in light of the benefits to law enforcement that accrue through CP. The Committee will closely monitor how CP requests are handled in the future and whether the low number of CP grants can be attributed to policy, practice, or some other reason.[14]

The bill includes protections related to unaccompanied immigrant minors. It builds on the successful "Child Advocate Program," which protects child trafficking victims and other children with protection-based claims. The bill also ensures that children who reach the age of maturity while in immigration custody are screened for vulnerabilities prior to being transferred to adult immigration detention. The bill offers a limited level of assistance to minors who were formerly considered unaccompanied minors, but later granted "U" visas because they were victims of crime who assisted law enforcement. The low cost of these programs are offset by the much greater reduction in authorizations contained in the bill.

Other significant changes in this reauthorization include additional law enforcement tools and resources to fight human trafficking crimes. For example, child exploitation laws under 18 U.S.C. § 2423 are strengthened to hold criminally liable those U.S. citizens and lawful permanent residents residing outside of the United States who engage in illicit sexual conduct with a minor. Current law only reaches U.S. citizens and lawful permanent residents who travel abroad in foreign commerce.

The bill adds a new misdemeanor provision as 18 U.S.C. § 1597, which criminalizes the unlawful confiscation or destruction of a person's immigration documents in order to maintain or restrict

---

[13] *See* Department of Homeland Security, "Continued Presence: Temporary Immigration Status for Victims of Human Trafficking" (August 2010); *see also,* http://www.dhs.gov/files/programs/gc_1284411607501.shtm.

[14] Contrary to the implication in the Additional Views from Senator Grassley, the Committee Report does not suggest that S. 1301 modifies the legal standard for Continued Presence (CP), nor does the Report suggest that law enforcement officials "do not know how to do their jobs and that Congress and advocates know better." See Additional Views from Senator Grassley, at 23. Rather, the Report articulates the intent of Congress in establishing CP and restates the Department of Homeland Security's implementation guidelines for CP. The discussion of CP above concludes with the Committee's intention to fulfill its oversight obligations with regard to implementation of the statute. In addition, the comments regarding CP are directly related to the new requirement in section 221 of the bill that the Attorney General report on "the number of persons who have been granted continued presence . . . and any efforts being taken to reduce the adjudication and processing time."

the labor or services of that person. An analogous felony is found in 18 U.S.C. § 1592, which addresses similar conduct committed in the course of violating specified human trafficking crimes. And the bill expands the definition of a "racketeering activity" for the Racketeer Influenced Corrupt Organizations Act,[15] to include fraud in foreign labor contracting, pursuant to 18 U.S.C. § 1351.

The legislation continues to authorize the Attorney General to make grants pursuant to 42 U.S.C. § 14044c to State and local law enforcement agencies, and expands the scope to include training and resources to investigate all forms of severe human trafficking, whether sex or labor trafficking, and whether experienced by foreign or domestic, minor or adult victims.

The bill does not reauthorize specific funds for the FBI. That change is not intended to signal a desire to reduce the FBI's role in fighting human trafficking. Rather, it reflects the fact that the FBI's anti-human trafficking efforts are funded by its annual appropriations for salaries and expenses, and not through this specific authorization. This Committee strongly supports the critical role the FBI plays in investigating and prosecuting human trafficking cases and expects that it will receive the funding necessary to combat these horrible crimes.

II. HISTORY OF THE BILL AND COMMITTEE CONSIDERATION

A. INTRODUCTION OF THE BILL

The Trafficking Victims Protection Reauthorization Act of 2011 was introduced as S. 1301 on June 29, 2011, by Senators Leahy, Kerry, Brown of Massachusetts, Boxer, Cardin and Wyden. The bill was referred to the Committee on the Judiciary. Since the bill's introduction, Senators Akaka, Brown of Ohio, Burr, Casey, Cochran, Coons, Durbin, Feinstein, Franken, Gillibrand, Hagen, Heller, Isakson, Klobuchar, Landrieu, Merkley, Mikulski, Nelson of Florida, Portman, Rubio, Schumer, Stabenow, Tester, and Udall of Colorado have joined as cosponsors.

B. COMMITTEE CONSIDERATION

1. Hearings

The Senate Committee on the Judiciary held a hearing titled, "The Trafficking Victims Protection Reauthorization Act: Renewing the Commitment to Victims of Human Trafficking," on September 14, 2011. The witnesses at the hearing were Mary Lou Leary, Principal Deputy Assistant Attorney General for the Office of Justice Programs of the Department of Justice; Luis CdeBaca, Ambassador-at-Large for the Office to Monitor and Combat Trafficking in Persons of the Department of State; and Kelly Ryan, Acting Deputy Assistant Secretary for Immigration and Border Security of the Department of Homeland Security. The witness testimony is available at http://www.judiciary.senate.gov/hearings/hearing.cfm?id=6344ca9cdcac94c57d1fa7ad3d740a6f.

2. Executive Business Meetings

The bill was placed on the Committee's agenda for consideration on October 2, 2011. It was held over on that date.

---

[15] 18 U.S.C. § 1961.

On October 13, 2011, the Committee on the Judiciary considered S. 1301. Chairman Leahy offered a Leahy-Grassley substitute amendment to the bill. The amendment was adopted by unanimous consent.

Senator Cornyn offered an amendment to strike sections of the bill relating to pilot programs for domestic minor sex trafficking and replace them with the text of the Domestic Minor Sex Trafficking Deterrence and Victims Support Act of 2010. The amendment was rejected by a roll call vote.

The vote record is as follows:

Tally: 7 Yeas, 11 Nays

Yeas (7): Hatch (R–UT), Kyl (R–AZ), Sessions (R–AL), Graham (R–SC), Cornyn (R–TX), Lee (R–UT), Coburn (R–OK).

Nays (11): Kohl (D–WI), Feinstein (D–CA), Schumer (D–NY), Durbin (D–IL), Whitehouse (D–RI), Klobuchar (D–MN), Franken (D–MN), Coons (D–DE), Blumenthal (D–CT), Grassley (R–IA), Leahy (D–VT).

Senator Blumenthal offered an amendment to require enhanced reporting by the Department of Defense of trafficking in persons claims and violations, including claims and violations by contractors. The amendment was accepted by a voice vote.

The Committee then voted to report S. 1301, the Trafficking Victims Protection Reauthorization Act, as amended, favorably to the Senate. The Committee proceeded by roll call vote as follows:

Tally: 12 Yeas, 6 Nays

Yeas (12): Kohl (D–WI), Feinstein (D–CA), Schumer (D–NY), Durbin (D–IL), Whitehouse (D–RI), Klobuchar (D–MN), Franken (D–MN), Coons (D–DE), Blumenthal (D–CT), Grassley (R–IA), Hatch (R–UT), Leahy (D–VT).

Nays (6): Kyl (R–AZ), Sessions (R–AL), Graham (R–SC), Cornyn (R–TX), Lee (R–UT), Coburn (R–OK).

III. SECTION-BY-SECTION SUMMARY OF THE BILL

TITLE I—COMBATING INTERNATIONAL TRAFFICKING IN PERSONS

Sec. 101. Regional strategies for combating trafficking in persons

This section requires regional bureaus of the Department of State to work in conjunction with the Office to Monitor and Combat Trafficking in Persons to formulate bilateral anti-trafficking goals and objectives. This section aims to ensure that communication with foreign government counterparts on trafficking occurs early in the reporting period and often, that the process is used to increase diplomacy with foreign governments on the issue, and that a uniform practice across bureaus and embassies is established.

Sec. 102. Regional Anti-Trafficking officers

This section authorizes the appointment of anti-trafficking officers based out of U.S. embassies to cover regions where human trafficking is most prevalent and foreign governmental efforts insufficient.

Sec. 103. Partnerships against significant trafficking in persons

This section re-orders existing language from sections 105 and 106 of the Trafficking Victims Protection Act of 2000 on "partnerships" and provides new tools and authorities for the Department of State to cooperate with the private sector, civil society, and foreign governments to combat human trafficking. It also promotes partnerships between foreign governments and non-governmental entities, and further authorizes the Secretary of State to establish an emergency fund to assist foreign governments in meeting unexpected, urgent needs related to human trafficking. Finally, it authorizes new cooperative funding mechanisms for technical assistance to foreign governments through "Child Protection Compacts" with selected eligible countries. S. 1301 does not increase authorization levels for this mechanism, but the Committee intends that the mechanism be used to partner with foreign governments toward transparent and measurable objectives.

Sec. 104. Protection and assistance for victims of trafficking

This section requires an annual Congressional briefing on State Department and United States Agency for International Development efforts to promote regional inter-governmental cooperation regarding victim protection and assistance, as well as criminal investigations and prosecutions.

Sec. 105. Minimum standards for the elimination of trafficking

This section amends the current minimum standards by which the Department of State measures efforts to eliminate human trafficking by including criteria relating to: (1) preventing human trafficking by nationals deployed in diplomatic missions alongside peacekeeping missions; (2) emphasizing the need for governments to have a transparent system for appropriately addressing a public official's involvement in human trafficking; (3) increasing inter-governmental cooperation and partnerships on a bilateral, multilateral, or regional basis, and with civil society; and (4) regulating foreign labor recruiters and criminalizing fraudulent recruiting.

Sec. 106. Best practices in trafficking in persons eradication

This section codifies the State Department's established practice of submitting a comprehensive annual report to Congress on governmental efforts to fight human trafficking, also known as the Trafficking in Persons Report. The Committee intends that the Department continue its practice of including the United States in the annual report. This section also codifies the State Department's existing practice of publishing on its website the rationale for any exercise of waiver authority under the category of "Countries on the Special Watch List for 2 Consecutive Years." This section also recommends consistency in the Department's inclusion of a section in the annual report highlighting exemplary governments and practices in the eradication of human trafficking.

This section also creates a new mechanism whereby countries selected for the "Tier 2" category that have made exemplary progress within this category will be mentioned as such. Wide disparity exists between the achievements of governments selected for Tier 2, and this section provides the Department of State with tools to mention high performing Tier 2 countries, not simply those whose efforts have been notably weak and, consequently, selected for "Tier 2 Watch List." While such governments progress may not merit inclusion in the "Tier 1" category, the Committee believes it may be beneficial to recognize strong "Tier 2" governments in order to encourage them to continue investing in successful anti-trafficking efforts.

Lastly, this section removes the authorization for the Secretary to produce and publish "interim reports"in order to reduce unnecessary or inefficient reporting.

Sec. 107. Protections for domestic workers and other non-immigrants

This section calls for the creation of an informative video for consular waiting rooms in countries with a high concentration of non-immigrant visa applications in addition to already existing pamphlets. While innovative implementation of this section is welcome, the requirement only applies to consular waiting rooms that currently have video capabilities and could be satisfied with a basic video with voiceovers dubbed in the appropriate language.

Sec. 108. Prevention of child trafficking through child marriage

This section requires the Secretary of State, in consultation with the Administrator of the United States Agency for International Development and relevant offices and bureaus, to formulate and distribute guidance to prevent child marriage and promote the empowerment of girls at risk of child marriage in developing countries. It also requires the annual State Department Country Reports on Human Rights Practices to include reporting on child marriage.

Sec. 109. Child soldiers

This section amends the prohibition on certain funds as established per Section 404(a) of the William Wilberforce Trafficking Victims Protection Reauthorization Act of 2008 by adding Peacekeeping Operations funds to existing limitations on providing U.S. security assistance to countries known to use child soldiers. The provision includes a Presidential waiver and exceptions for efforts to professionalize forces and reduce the use of child soldiers within militaries in question.

Sec. 110. Presidential award for technological innovations in trafficking in persons eradication

This section adds "technological innovation" to the bases upon which the President may select an honoree for the "Presidential Award for Extraordinary Efforts to Combat Trafficking in Persons."

Sec. 111. Contracting requirements

This section helps to prevent labor and sex trafficking by government contractors and subcontractors. It expands an existing provision under the TVPA to require the government to include a condition in every contract, grant, or cooperative agreement that authorizes the Federal department or agency to terminate a contract if the contractor or subcontractor engages in acts related to trafficking, has procured a commercial sex act, or uses forced labor in the performance of the grant, contract, or cooperative agreement.

The Committee recommends that all Federal departments or agencies apply these conditions when negotiating agreements with Non-Appropriated Funding Instrumentalities and Military Morale, Welfare, and Recreation Programs including the Army Air Force Exchange (AAFES) and Navy Exchange.

This section specifically authorizes contract termination in a number of instances, including if an employer destroys or removes an employee's immigration documents without the employee's consent, or fails to assist with repatriation of the employee after the end of employment. This provision is not intended to supplant existing requirements that place full responsibility for employee repatriation on the employer. It also authorizes contract termination if the employer places the recruited employee in a location or work placement different from that promised when the employee is recruited. This provision is intended to both prevent employers from misrepresenting location and occupation information during employee recruitment and to prevent employers from economically coercing recruited individuals to consent to a change in location or occupation after the employee has left his or her host country. This section also authorizes termination of a contract upon the charging of placement fees equal to or greater than the annual salary or half the employee's total anticipated pay, whichever is less. The Committee recognizes that other excessive or exorbitant placement fees may be grounds for contract termination and did not intend to relieve contractors from compliance with host country laws or contract representations and certifications. Finally, the section authorizes termination for any other activities that support or promote trafficking in persons, the procurement of commercial sex, or forced labor in order to give contracting officers greater latitude to terminate a contract for reasons not specifically listed in subsections A–D.

This section also requires contractors to create a compliance plan to prevent activities related to trafficking in persons, procurement of commercial sex, or forced labor, and to certify upon due diligence that neither the contractor nor any subcontractors are engaged in such activities. Upon the receipt of credible reports of noncompliance, the contracting officer is authorized, depending on the extent of the violation, to attempt to resolve the noncompliance, modify the existing agreement, decline to renew the agreement, or terminate the agreement. Credible reports include, but are not limited to, reports from a contracting officer representative, an inspector general, an auditor, or any other official source, which may include a victim of trafficking.

Sec. 112. Department of Defense reporting of trafficking in persons claims and violations

This section requires the Department of Defense to make public information on all known trafficking cases through the annual report to Congress of the Interagency Task Force to Monitor and Combat Trafficking.

TITLE II—COMBATING TRAFFICKING IN PERSONS IN THE UNITED STATES

Subtitle A—Penalties Against Traffickers and Other Crimes

Sec. 201. Criminal trafficking offenses

This section modifies criminal law provisions that address trafficking in persons. First, under the Racketeer Influenced Corrupt Organizations Act (18 U.S.C. § 1961), the definition of a "racketeering activity" is expanded to include fraud in foreign labor contracting, pursuant to 18 U.S.C. § 1351.

Second, child exploitation laws under 18 U.S.C. § 2423 are strengthened to hold criminally liable those U.S. citizens and lawful permanent residents residing outside of the United States who engage in illicit sexual conduct with a minor. Current law only reaches U.S. citizens and lawful permanent residents who travel abroad in foreign commerce.

Third, a new misdemeanor provision is added as 18 U.S.C. § 1597, which criminalizes the unlawful confiscation or destruction of a person's immigration documents in order to maintain or restrict the labor or services of that person. An analogous felony is found in 18 U.S.C. § 1592, which addresses similar conduct committed in the course of violating or with intent to violate specified human trafficking crimes.

Sec. 202. Civil remedies, clarifying definition

This section expands civil remedies available to minor victims under 18 U.S.C. § 2255. Current law allows minor victims to file suit for damages if the minor was a victim of a sexual abuse or exploitation crime as defined in chapters 109A and 110 of Title 18. The amended section allows minors who were victims of a severe form of trafficking in persons to recover civil damages under this section. It also increases the civil statute of limitations for all minors who file suit under 18 U.S.C. § 2255 from six years to ten years. Additionally, the existing criminal law definition of "abuse or threatened abuse of law or legal process" from 18 U.S.C. §§ 1589 and 1591 is added to the general definitions of the Trafficking Victims Protection Act of 2000.

Subtitle B—Ensuring Availability of Possible Witnesses and Informants

Sec. 211. Protections for threatened family members of trafficking victims

This section modestly augments the list of eligible relatives who may file as a derivative beneficiary of a "T" visa holder. The section would allow children of certain derivative family members to apply to join the trafficking victim in the United States, but only if those children face a present danger of retaliation in their home country by the traffickers. Children of derivative family members who do not face retaliation would not be eligible.

Sec. 212. Encouraging victims of fraud in foreign labor contracting to assist law enforcement

This section adds "fraud in foreign labor contracting," as defined by 18 U.S.C. §1351, to the list of crimes of which victims may be eligible to apply for a "U" visa. (See INA § 101(a)(15)(U); 8 U.S.C. §1101(a)(15)(U). "U" visa recipients must show that they are victims of a qualifying criminal activity, have suffered substantial physical or mental abuse as a result of that crime, and are willing to assist law enforcement or other government officials in the investigation or prosecution of the crime. "U" visa recipients are not eligible for any Federal benefits. Fraud in foreign labor contracting is difficult to prosecute because victims are often reluctant to come forward and report the crime for fear of being deported. Including this crime as a qualifying criminal activity for a "U" visa will encourage greater reporting and prosecution of this offense.

Subtitle C—Ensuring Inter-Agency Coordination and Expanded Reporting

Sec. 221. Reporting requirements by the Attorney General

Under current law, the Attorney General is required to submit an annual report to Congress detailing efforts by Federal agencies to implement the Trafficking Victims Protection Act. In order to more accurately determine the effectiveness of those efforts, this section requires the Attorney General to also report on how efficiently "T" and "U" visas are processed, efforts to train State, Tribal, and local law enforcement on investigating human trafficking crimes, and how Federal programs meet the needs of minor victims of trafficking who are U.S. citizens or lawful permanent residents.

Sec. 222. Reporting requirements by the Secretary of Labor

TVPRA 2005 required the Department of Labor to monitor and make efforts to combat forced and child labor in foreign countries, including making public a list of foreign goods produced by forced or child labor. This section requires the Secretary of Labor to provide that list to Congress biannually.

Sec. 223. Information sharing to combat child labor and slave labor

In order to assist the Department of Labor in compiling the list of goods produced by forced or child labor referenced in section 223 (above), this section directs the Department of State to provide relevant information to the Department of Labor.

Sec. 224. Government training efforts to include the Department of Labor

This section expands the number of agencies required to be trained in indentifying victims of a severe form of trafficking to include certain personnel from the Department of Labor.

Sec. 225. GAO report on the use of foreign labor contractors

To ensure that foreign workers contracted to work in or for the United States do not suffer abuses or are not fraudulently recruited by third-party brokers or subcontractors, this section directs the GAO to issue a report investigating whether any such foreign workers were subjected to abuse or trafficking. The report would analyze the current contracting system and make recommendations to Federal agencies to rectify any known abuses.

Sec. 226. Oversight of Department of Justice Grant Program

This section adds a number of audits and oversight requirements on grants awarded by the Department of Justice (DOJ). It adds caps on administrative expenses and matching requirements for DOJ grants. It limits conference expenditures and prohibits lobbying from being conducted with government funds, among other measures.

Subtitle D—Enhancing State and Local Efforts to Combat Trafficking in Persons

Sec. 231. Assistance for domestic minor sex trafficking victims

This section replaces a services grant program with a block grant program administered by the Department of Justice to four localities that have demonstrated a comprehensive approach in addressing sex trafficking of minors, including cooperation between law enforcement and social service providers. The localities may distribute the grants to entities that provide, among other things, residential care, emergency social services, and mental health counseling. The authorized appropriations do not change. Additionally, this section saves $5,000,000 by not reauthorizing a pilot program under the Department of Health and Human Services.

Sec. 232. Expanding local law enforcement grants for investigations and prosecutions of sex trafficking

Under current law, 42 U.S.C. § 14044c authorizes the Attorney General to make grants to State and local law enforcement agencies to provide training and resources to investigate trafficking in persons. This section requires the provision to focus on all forms of severe human trafficking. In an effort to attack the demand side of sex trafficking, it also encourages efforts to prosecute individuals who purchase commercial sex acts from minors, along with the traffickers. This section also includes a mandate for GAO to evaluate the program and reduces authorization levels by $10,000,000.

Sec. 233. Model state law protection for child trafficking victims and survivors

This section amends Section 225(b) of the Trafficking Victims Protection Reauthorization Act of 2008 to encourage the Attorney General to develop model code language for States that would treat children exploited through prostitution as victims, not criminals.

TITLE III—AUTHORIZATIONS OF APPROPRIATIONS

Sec. 301. Adjust authorization levels of provision of the Trafficking Victims Protection Act of 2000

This section details the changes to the authorization of appropriations that were originally enacted by the Trafficking Victims Protection Act of 2000. Overall, S. 1301 reduces authorization levels by more than $60 million annually compared to the Trafficking Victims Protection Reauthorization Act of 2008. In this section, the authorization levels for the Departments of State, Homeland Security, and Labor, as well as the Federal Bureau of Investigation, have been reduced. At the same time, authorization of appropriations for victim benefits and services administered by the Department of Health and Human Services and by the Department of Justice are increased by $3,000,000 and $5,000,000 respectively. Authorizations for additional personnel and reception expenses have been removed.

Sec. 302. *Adjust authorization levels of provisions of the Trafficking Victims Protection Reauthorization Act of 2005*

The appropriations listed in this section reduce previously authorized levels of funding for conferences and a pilot program of the U.S. Agency for International Development.

TITLE IV—UNACCOMPANIED ALIEN CHILDREN

Sec. 401. *Appropriate custodial settings for unaccompanied minors who reach the age of majority while in Federal custody*

This section modifies Section 235(c)(2) of the TVPRA 2008 to address the situation of unaccompanied minors in the custody of the Office of Refugee Resettlement who reach the age of 18 prior to resolution of their immigration case. Such persons are typically transferred to adult immigration detention under the authority of U.S. Immigration and Customs Enforcement (ICE). This section requires the Secretary to consider placement of the individual in the least restrictive setting available after taking into consideration the individual's danger to self, danger to the community, and risk of flight. The Secretary would retain discretion to place an immigrant in a detention facility if deemed necessary for public safety.

Sec. 402. *Appointment of child advocates for unaccompanied minors*

This section would expand the successful Child Advocate program that was established as a pilot program in 2003. Child Advocates are independent actors who assist trafficking victims and other vulnerable immigrant children by ensuring immediate and long-term welfare and access to protection, consistent with the child's best interests. This section would expand the current Child Advocate program from its current operations (a program in Chicago, IL, and limited offerings in Harlingen, TX) to three additional locations within the next two years, with locations selected based on the greatest need. Within four years, the program can be expanded to an additional three sites. This section requires reporting to Congress by the Secretary of Health and Human Services and a GAO study on the effectiveness of the Child Advocate program. This section authorizes $1,000,000 per year for each of the first two years of the reauthorization and $2,000,000 for each of years three and four of the reauthorization. To ensure effective management of Federal funds, this section imposes a cap of 10% on administrative expenses and also requires the Child Advocate program to match the Federal funds received at a rate of 25%.

Sec. 403. *Access to Federal foster care and unaccompanied refugee minor protections for certain U visa recipients*

Under current law, when an unaccompanied immigrant minor who was also a victim of crime is awarded a "U" visa, that minor loses eligibility for certain benefits available to children who are considered unaccompanied minors under law. No benefits attach to "U" visa status. This section would make "U" visa recipients who are minors and who were formerly considered unaccompanied minors eligible for Federal foster care and certain benefits available to refugee minors. This provision would not apply to all "U" visa recipients who happen to be minors, but only to the small number of minor victims who were formerly deemed unaccompanied under law.

Sec. 404. Study of the effectiveness of border screenings under section 235(a)(4) of the William Wilberforce Trafficking Victims Protection Reauthorization Act of 2008

This section requires GAO to conduct a study on the implementation of provisions of TVPRA 2008 with regard to Department of Homeland Security (DHS) screening of children. For example, GAO will assess whether DHS personnel are adequately screening children to determine whether they may be victims of trafficking or persecution. GAO will also assess whether children are properly cared for while in the custody of the DHS and repatriated in an appropriate manner.

IV. Congressional Budget Office Cost Estimate

The cost estimate provided by the Congressional Budget Office pursuant to section 402 of the Congressional Budget Act of 1974 was not available for inclusion in this report. The estimate will be printed in either a supplemental report or the Congressional Record when it is available.

V. Regulatory Impact Evaluation

In compliance with rule XXVI of the Standing Rules of the Senate, the Committee finds that no significant regulatory impact will result from the enactment of S. 1301.

VI. Conclusion

Much progress has been made since the Trafficking Victims Protection Act was signed into law in 2000 to combat the scourge of human trafficking in the United States and around the world. Nonetheless, millions of people worldwide continue to be victimized by this modern form of slavery. The Trafficking Victims Protection Reauthorization Act of 2011 reaffirms our country's commitment to fight modern day slavery and exploitation. It continues and strengthens programs that are working well and gives law enforcement additional tools to target trafficking. It also reduces authorization levels and builds in accountability measures to ensure that scarce Federal funds are being well spent. The Committee believes that Congress should come together, as it has done several times before with overwhelming support, to make progress in the fight against trafficking and pass this important legislation.

VII. ADDITIONAL AND MINORITY VIEWS

ADDITIONAL VIEWS FROM SENATOR GRASSLEY

Federal government efforts to combat human trafficking are worthy and appropriate. Human trafficking is a terrible crime and those who commit this crime must be prosecuted to the fullest extent of the law. In addressing this topic, Congress passed and President Clinton signed into law the Trafficking Victims Protection Act (TVPA) in 2000. The original TVPA, and the subsequent reauthorizations, have all recognized the horrific nature of these crimes and have received significant bi-partisan support. In this vein, I worked hard to negotiate a bi-partisan compromise with the Chairman to ensure that this important law is reauthorized. The final version of S. 1301 contains a number of changes that I requested and believe strengthen the program while recognizing the difficult financial times the Country faces. These changes help to reduce unnecessary and duplicative expenditures, consolidate funding streams to mirror actual appropriations, and ensure that there is accountability and oversight of grant recipients. Together, these changes will help to ensure the sustainability of funding for prevention of human trafficking.

While I support the final version of the bill, I have some concerns with the interpretations of it as articulated by the Committee report. These additional views represent my understanding of the final compromise reached between the Chairman and myself and offer further details on important provisions I worked to include as part of the final compromise.

Concerns with human trafficking statistics

More than ten years after the passage of TVPA, there is still no reliable information about the scope of this criminal activity. In an audit released in 2006, the Government Accountability Office (GAO) stated, "The U.S. government has not yet established an effective mechanism for estimating the number of victims or for conducting ongoing analysis of trafficking related data that resides within various government agencies." [1] In the five years since then, there has been no improvement in the government's ability to quantify the data related to this crime, in particular the number of victims, both in the United States and around the world. Only with valid figures—or at least evidence-based estimates—can we be sure that the funds spent on the fight against trafficking are having the impact they are intended to have.

---

[1] U.S. Gov't Accountability Office, "Human Trafficking: Better Data, Strategy, and Reporting Needed to Enhance U.S. Trafficking Efforts Abroad," GAO–06–825 (July 2006), p. 18.

According to the latest Department of Justice (DOJ) figures available to the Committee, there were only about 2000 victims discovered in the United States from Fiscal Year 2001 to 2009.[2] Figures for FY 2010 are not available because DOJ has still not delivered the statutorily mandated report on efforts to combat trafficking that was due to Congress in May of 2011. Likewise, according to the State Department's annual Trafficking in Persons report, there were only 33,000 victims identified around the world last year.[3] These figures contrast sharply with estimates provided in the past by the Executive Branch and frequently cited by various interest groups and the media such as 14,500 to 17,000 thousand in the United States each year and 600,000 to 800,000 around the globe each year. As the GAO put it in 2006, "There is significant discrepancy between the number of estimated victims and the number of observed victims . . ."[4]

The State Department acknowledged this fact itself in its 2010 Trafficking in Persons Report, where it reported that only 0.4 percent of estimated victims had been identified.[5] While it is reasonable to assume that because of the underground nature of trafficking, many victims are kept hidden from authorities and are difficult to find and rescue, at the same time, the worldwide focus on trafficking for more than 10 years should have led to better identification of victims by now. In particular, the figure for United States victims identified and rescued should be quite high. But, taking the lower end of the estimate of victims in the United States, it is simply not credible that, given the amount of federal resources devoted to the problem, only 2,000 of 150,000 victims, or slightly more than 1 percent, have been found in the last 11 years. Either the government is doing an unconscionably poor job of finding victims or there are not that many total victims in the first place. It is my hope, that this reauthorization will lead to better reporting on the true number of victims and will help jumpstart more accurate reporting on human trafficking statistics to Congress and the American people. At the least, DOJ should be on notice going forward that continuing to turn in reports to Congress months late is unacceptable, especially when Congress is attempting to reauthorize important legislation impacting their operations.

Continued presence

First, it must be clear that this bill makes no changes to the law pertaining to Continued Presence (CP). The law, found in 22 U.S.C. § 7105(c)(3)(A)(i), provides: "[i]f a Federal law enforcement official files an application stating that an alien is a victim of a severe form of trafficking and may be a potential witness to such trafficking, the Secretary of Homeland Security may permit the alien to remain in the United States to facilitate the investigation and prosecution of those responsible for such crime." Any interpretation articulated in the Committee Report cannot affect the current status of the CP law or how it is administered. And, because this leg-

[2] Dep't of Justice, Attorney General's Annual Report to Congress and Assessment of U.S. Government Efforts to Combat Trafficking in Persons, Fiscal Year 2009 (May 2010), p. 20.
[3] Department of State, Trafficking in Persons Report 2011 (June 2011), p. 38.
[4] Gov't Accountability Office, *supra* Note 1, at p. 17.
[5] Department of State, Trafficking in Persons Report 2010 (June 2010), p. 7.

islation in no way alters the current statutory standard for CP, neither the Executive Branch, nor the courts, should view opinions contained in this report as changing the legal standard in any way.

Second, the Committee Report also discusses DHS guidelines describing when CP should be used. It declares that "[t]his decline [in the number of individuals receiving CP] is troubling, especially in light of the benefits to law enforcement that accrue through CP." The report concludes its discussion of CP by stating: "The Committee will closely monitor how CP requests are handled in the future and whether the low number of CP grants can be attributed to policy, practice, or some other reason." It appears that these statements are meant to imply that law enforcement and prosecutors do not know how to do their jobs and that Congress and advocates know better. I disagree with this implication.

As the DHS guidelines, relied upon by the report, make clear: "CP is an important tool for federal, state, and local law enforcement in their investigation of human trafficking-related crimes."[6] Consequently, whether, when, and how often to use CP is a matter for law enforcement and prosecutors to determine on a case-by-case basis, using their expertise. The Committee has not been presented with any evidence that law enforcement officers and prosecutors are not properly enforcing trafficking laws. Nor has the Committee been presented with any evidence that they are not appropriately utilizing CP.

Indeed, on October 3, 2011, the Committee's majority staff organized a briefing by five local law enforcement officials on the use of U-Visas (for victims of crime), T-Visas (for victims of trafficking) and Violence Against Women Act (VAWA) self-petitions. The declared purpose of the briefing was to provide useful background information to staff as the Committee considered the Trafficking Victims Protection Reauthorization Act (S. 1301) and the VAWA Reauthorization. The law enforcement officials were described by the majority staff as having significant experience working to fight domestic violence, sexual violence, and trafficking in their communities, and training other law enforcement officers on the use of U visas as a law enforcement tool. During that briefing, none of the officers indicated that there were any problems with the standard for requesting CP or the frequency in which CP requests are made.

Generally speaking, career law enforcement officers and prosecutors know how to do their jobs and do not, as a general matter, need to be told how to fight crime. To date, there has been no evidence presented to suggest that career law enforcement officers and prosecutors are failing to utilize CP as a crime fighting tool.

In the end, the standard for CP is set forth in 22 U.S.C. § 7105(c)(3)(A)(i). The TVPRA does not change that standard. And, interpretations contained in this report cannot and do not change that standard.

Funding provisions of TVPA

Chief among the key provisions of the TVPA has been the authorizations that provide funding to many different programs to

---

[6] Dep't of Homeland Security, Continued Presence: Temporary Immigration Status for Victims of Human Trafficking (August 2010) (available at http://www.dhs.gov/files/programs/gc_1284411607501.shtm).

combat human trafficking. These provisions have previously authorized funding to the Department of Justice, Department of State, Department of Homeland Security, Department of Labor, Department of Health and Human Services, and the Executive Office of the President. The past versions of TVPA had created approximately twenty-six separate budgetary line items that authorized $191.5 million annually. Because funding for TVPA programs was stretched across so many different accounts, there has been significant duplication, overlap, and unnecessary expenditures under TVPA funded programs.

For example, the 2005 TVPA Reauthorization included a $30 million funding stream for the Federal Bureau of Investigation (FBI) to investigate trafficking in persons.[7] This funding was included to specifically recognize the importance of investigating trafficking in person's cases. While I agree with the goal of this additional funding, to continue this additional authorization, on top of the nearly $7.8 billion the FBI received in Fiscal Year 2011, is duplicative. Further, this provision has never been funded by the appropriators. In fact, the Fiscal Year 2012 Senate Subcommittee on Commerce, Justice, Science, and Related Agencies Appropriations specifically included language in the Fiscal Year 2012 Committee Report that states, "Within funds provided, the Committee expects the FBI to investigate severe forms of trafficking in persons as authorized by [the TVPA]." This statement essentially indicates that the appropriations staff view the duty to investigate severe forms of trafficking in persons as part of the inherent duty of the FBI that does not require specific, additional funding. Given the unprecedented fiscal situation the federal government faces, along with traditional principles of good government, the compromise version of S. 1301 eliminates the specific line item for additional funds for the FBI.

Following the same principles of good government, and continuing to recognize the extraordinary fiscal times the federal government faces, the final compromise of S. 1301 that I supported reduces the overall funding levels for TVPA programs, from $191.5 million per year to approximately $130 million per year. To achieve this significant reduction, significant time and resources were paid to reviewing each of the programs previously authorized and funded to determine where duplication, overlap, waste, and unnecessary expenditures existed. This review highlighted ten funding streams that were not reauthorized, including the special FBI funding previously discussed. This includes eliminating "reception" expenses at the State Department, two pilot programs that were never funded, two overlapping studies at the Justice Department, funding for research and foreign assistance in the Executive Office of the President that is duplicative and overlaps with State Department funding, and eliminating a local grant program at HHS. Further, the final compromise also significantly reduces, but does not eliminate, expenditures for DHS and the State Department.

While cutting budgets is often difficult given the institutional opposition to eliminating programs, making tough choices in these programs was necessary. Those difficult choices allowed us to increase funding to victims of severe forms of trafficking by increas-

---

[7] Pub. L. No. 109–164, 119 Stat. 3558, 301(7), Jan. 10, 2006.

ing funding to the Department of Justice's victims assistance programs. Taken together, the final compromise strikes the right balance in eliminating duplicative and unappropriated programs while funding programs that are worthy—such as assistance to victims of severe forms of trafficking.

Accountability and transparency measures

Perhaps the most important part of the final compromise of S. 1301 is the inclusion of a strong accountability package to ensure that taxpayer dollars are not subject to fraud, waste, and abuse. By reducing or eliminating fraud, waste, and abuse, we ensure that victims are receiving all of the services and assistance that our authorizations intend. This accountability package, located in section 226, contains a number of different measures that will help eliminate the past abuses of TVPA grant programs.

At the hearing in September, I questioned the Principal Deputy Assistant Attorney General for the Office of Justice Programs—one of two offices that provides grant funding under TVPA programs. During that questioning, I discussed how in the past four years, the Inspector General at the Justice Department has audited seven individual grant recipients under the TVPA. Each of those seven audits contained significant irregularities including unallowable costs, unauthorized expenditures, poor accounting and financial records, failure of programs to meet stated goals, and failure to provide matching funds identified in grant applications. The Inspector General found "systemic weaknesses in [OJP's] grant implementation," including "weaknesses in the areas of the established goals and accomplishments for grantees, grant reporting, fund drawdowns, local matching funds, expenditures, indirect costs, and monitoring of subrecepients." [8] In one instance, a grantee was given nearly $2 million for human trafficking assistance, and the Inspector General questioned nearly $900,000, plus an additional $174,000 in fringe benefits.[9] The Principal Deputy Assistant Attorney General agreed with my analysis that this grant was an example of a spectacular failure on the part of the government to oversee taxpayer dollars.[10] Unfortunately, I was then told what I have been told for years, that the Justice Department has fixed this problem and that it won't happen again.

Despite repeated assurances that the Justice Department is doing more now than it has in the past to prevent fraud, waste, and abuse of taxpayer dollars, the song remains the same. Grant recipients continue to commit major program violations and yet continue to receive taxpayer dollars year after year. For example, in a January 2008 audit report, the OIG questioned "all expenditures in salaries ($902,122) and in fringe benefits ($174,479) due to the lack of adequate supporting documentation." [11] The OIG also questioned, "$70,580 for . . . unsupported matching contributions

---

[8] Dep't of Justice, Office of Inspector General, Management of the Office of Justice Programs' Grant Programs for Trafficking Victims, OIG Audit Report 08–26 (July 2008).

[9] Dep't of Justice, Office of Inspector General, Legal Assistance for Victims Grant and Services for Human Trafficking Victims Grants Administered by the Heartland Alliance for Human Needs and Human Rights, Chicago, Illinois OIG Audit Report GR–50–08–002 (January 2008)

[10] The Trafficking Victims Protection Reauthorization Act: Renewing the Commitment to Victims of Human Trafficking: Hearing before the Senate Comm. on the Judiciary, Sept. 14, 2011.

[11] See Dep't of Justice supra note 8.

for salary and fringe benefits," as well as "$63,009 in expenditures that exceeded the maximum daily rate [for pro bono legal service matching requirements]." [12] Another January 2008 audit of a law enforcement task force found "that the grantee generally complied with grant requirements", but the OIG also "found that an unauthorized position was charged to the grant," and that the grantee "maintained an accounting system and financial records that did not always account for grant-related expenditures and revenue." [13] A March 2008 grant audit of a New York-based recipient also found significant weaknesses in grant expenditures. For example, the OIG found that the grantee was "not achieving the objectives pertaining to social services and legal services because it was not serving 100 victims, and did not obtain 80 T-visas for victims on trafficking identified during the project period as budgeted." [14] The OIG also found weaknesses in how the grantee determined client eligibility for services; identified the number of clients served; failed to provide supporting documentation for housing costs; paying in full for contracts for housing, medical, and legal services for victims despite serving fewer victims than contracted, and complied with the matching requirements. In all, the OIG questioned nearly $500,000 of the original $2 million grant. [15] In addition to these individual audits, the Inspector General has questioned the number of victims that the Office of Justice Program's anti-trafficking efforts have served. [16] That same audit, found "systematic weaknesses in [OJP's] grant implementation" citing the need for the Office of Victims of Crime (OVC) and the Bureau of Justice Assistance (BJA) to take "additional actions to ensure that these weaknesses are addressed by all OVC service providers and BJS [Bureau of Justice Statistics] task forces, not just the subjects of the individual audits we conducted." Thus, not only has the OIG questioned the administration of TVPA grants by individual grant recipients, the OIG has questioned the actual administration of the grant programs both by BJA and OVW.

The GAO has also issued two separate reports criticizing BJA and the entire U.S. Government effort to coordinate programs under TVPA. [17] These audits and evaluations show systemic problems that the OIG and GAO has found in other grant programs administered by OJP and other Justice components. In fact, grant management has been on the OIG's annual list of major management challenges for DOJ each year for the last ten years. Simply put, these audits are not an isolated incident and appear to be the rule, not the exception. Sadly, given the small sample of actual grantees audited on an annual basis, an accurate total of taxpayer

---

[12] *Id.*

[13] Dep't of Justice, Office of Inspector General, Office of Justice Programs, San Diego Region Anti-Trafficking Task Force Grant Awarded to County of San Diego California, OIG Audit Report GR–90–08–001 (January 2008).

[14] Dep't of Justice, Office of Inspector General, Office of Justice Programs, Office for Victims of Crime, Services for Trafficking Victims, Discretionary Grant Program, Cooperative Agreement Awarded to the International Rescue Comm, New York, New York OIG Audit Report GR–40–08–003 (March 2008).

[15] *Id.*

[16] Dep't of Justice *supra* note 8.

[17] Gov't Accountability *Supra* Note 1; U.S. Gov't Accountability Office, Human Trafficking: A Strategic Framework Could Help Enhance the Interagency Collaboration Needed to Effectively Combat Trafficking Crimes GAO–07–915 (July 2007).

dollars lost to fraud, waste, abuse, or mismanagement of grant programs cannot be calculated.

To combat these repeated negative audit findings, I prepared a significant accountability package that includes a number of measures to ensure that grants are actually audited and those who mismanage taxpayer dollars are held accountable. The final compromise version of S. 1301 includes the following accountability measures: (1) requires an annual audit of 10% of all grantees by the Inspector General, (2) requires a two-year exclusion for any grantee found to have an unresolved audit finding for more than six months, (3) requires the Attorney General to prioritize grants to grantees that do not have a negative audit finding for the last three fiscal years, (4) requires the Attorney General to reimburse the federal treasury if a barred grantee is awarded funds, then seek to recoup funds from the erroneous award to the grantee, (5) requires matching funds from grantees—including a limitation on in-kind contributions, (6) prohibits the Attorney General from awarding grants to any non-profit organization that holds money offshore for the purpose of avoiding unrelated business income tax (UBIT), (7) caps administrative expenses, (8) requires the Deputy Attorney General or Assistant Attorney General to pre-approve conference expenditures and annually report to Congress, (9) prohibits grantees from using taxpayer dollars to lobby for additional taxpayer funds, and (10) requires the Assistant Attorney General for the Office of Justice Programs to annually certify to Congress compliance with the mandatory exclusions and reimbursements contained in the bill.

These requirements are a commonsense proposal to ensure a baseline of accountability for federal grantees receiving funds under the TVPA. They are a response to problems that have arisen in the TVPA administered grant program, in addition to others—including reentry programs funded under the Second Chance Act, victims and law enforcement grants under the Violence Against Women Act, and many other grants administered by the OJP, the OVW, and the Community Oriented Policing Services (COPS). While the Committee Report argues that these accountability provisions are "specifically tailored to the needs and contours of the grant programs authorized under the TVPA", it is my belief that given the many similarities and overlapping problems with grants administered by DOJ, these accountability provisions cross programmatic boundaries and would establish a minimum baseline of accountability across all DOJ administered grant programs. Given the current fiscal crisis the federal government faces, and the continued findings of the OIG outlining fraud, waste, abuse, and mismanagement of DOJ administered grant programs, it is imperative that the Judiciary Committee undertake a comprehensive effort to include these accountability measures in some form to all reauthorizations of grant programs going forward.

Conclusion

Human trafficking is a horrific crime that requires the attention of the federal government and those who commit this terrible crime should be prosecuted to the fullest extent of the law. The final Committee reported version of S. 1301 represents a step forward for victims and American taxpayers. By reexamining the existing funding streams and determining where savings could be made, the bill was able to cut spending while simultaneously increase funding for victims. Additionally, by adding a significant accountability package, this bill signals to grant recipients that they too need to increase their efforts to better manage federal government resources in order to serve victims in a more efficient manner.

CHARLES E. GRASSLEY.

MINORITY VIEWS FROM SENATORS KYL, SESSIONS, LEE AND COBURN

Since passage of the Trafficking Victims Protection Act (TVPA) in 2000, Congress has regularly reauthorized and expanded programs to combat human trafficking. Although funding to combat this tragic crime has increased exponentially over the last decade, Congress has failed to provide the necessary oversight to ensure this money is being spent efficiently and effectively. As a direct result of this failure, there is now a growing bureaucracy of anti-trafficking programs that is wasteful, mismanaged, and duplicative. S. 1301, the Trafficking Victims Protection Reauthorization Act of 2011 (TVPRA), takes admirable steps to curb the amount of spending on anti-trafficking programs in light of the current economic climate; nevertheless, this legislation fails to implement necessary changes in the structure and design of these programs.

The amount of money authorized to combat human trafficking increased from $31.8 million in 2001 to $185.5 million in 2010. At the same time, the number of agencies and programs charged with combating trafficking rose dramatically: eight federal agencies now receive funding under the TVPA,[1] as well as countless programs, funds, and task forces. Unfortunately, Congress continues to neglect its duty to provide proper oversight of these various agencies and programs, and as a result a significant amount of the funding provided under the TVPA is wasted or mismanaged. Even worse, some of the agencies receiving this funding have difficulty merely keeping a proper account of their funds. While S. 1301 takes some initial, positive steps in reining in the waste and mismanagement of the various anti-trafficking programs by reducing their authorizations or eliminating programs that have not been appropriated in the past, the bill as currently written does not ensure we are effectively spending each dollar.

Imbalance between domestic and international program funding

The protection of American citizens from human trafficking, and the prosecution of those who attempt to engage in such trafficking in the United States, was the foremost concern of the initial Trafficking Victims Protection Act. However, the TVPA has evolved over time, and the protection of American citizens is no longer the central focus of the government's anti-trafficking efforts. Instead, U.S. Government programs focus on combating international trafficking and increasing public awareness in foreign countries. In FY2010, domestic anti-trafficking programs received only $24.2 million while international programs received more than $85 mil-

---

[1] Department of State, USAID, Department of Justice, Department of Labor, Department of Health and Human Services, Department of Homeland Security, Immigration and Customs Enforcement, and the Executive Office of the President.

lion; as a result, international programs accounted for 78% of the U.S. Government's TIP funding.[2] This gap in funding between domestic and international programs has been consistent over time—over the last three years, Congress appropriated $244.9 million to combat international trafficking while only appropriating $67 million to combat domestic trafficking.[3]

Furthermore, there is even confusion as to whether any funds provided under the TVPA may be used to supply direct services to U.S. citizen victims. The Attorney General's Annual Report to Congress and Assessment of U.S. Government Activities to Combat Trafficking in Persons issued on July 2010 states: "The funds provided under the TVPA by the federal government for direct services to victims are dedicated to assist non-U.S. citizen victims and may not be used to assist U.S. citizen victims."[4] In a December 2010 report, the Congressional Research Service noted this lack of clarity, stating: "There is confusion over whether U.S. citizens, as well as noncitizens, are eligible for services under all the anti-trafficking grant programs, and whether Congress has provided funding for programs that target U.S. citizen and LPR (lawful permanent resident) victims." Congress should alleviate this confusion and ensure assistance is being provided to U.S. citizens before providing grants to foreign countries; unfortunately, S. 1301 fails to do so. S. 1301 does not re-direct any funding from international programs to domestic programs, nor does it clarify that U.S. citizen victims may be the recipients of direct services under the TVPA. As a result, the TVPRA continues to disadvantage American citizens in favor of foreign governments.

Waste and duplication in international anti-trafficking programs

The TVPA's focus on international programs is especially problematic in view of these programs' deficiencies. For instance, one of the leading international anti-trafficking programs is the Office to Monitor and Combat Trafficking in Persons (G/TIP), an agency within the Department of State—in Fiscal Year 2010, G/TIP provided more than $33 million for anti-trafficking programs.[5] At the same time, the 2011 Department of State Report to the Senate Appropriations Committee included a startling admission: only 67% of all projects reporting to G/TIP could provide an accurate and detailed accounting of their funding and the proportion of said funding that directly assisted victims of trafficking crimes.[6] This figure

---

[2] "U.S. Government Anti-Trafficking In Persons Program Funding, FY2010 Fact Sheet." United States Department of State, *available at http://www.state.gov/documents/organization/167319.pdf.*

[3] Data from 2009–2011 "U.S. Government Anti-Trafficking In Persons Program Funding" Fact Sheets. United States Department of State, *available at http://www.state.gov/g/tip/rls/fs/index.htm.*

[4] "Attorney General's Annual Report to Congress and Assessment of U.S. Government Activities to Combat Trafficking in Persons, Fiscal Year 2009," at 17. *Available at http://www.justice.gov/ag/annualreports/tr2009/agreporthumantrafficking2009.pdf.*

[5] 2011 Department of State Report to the U.S. Senate Appropriations Committee, Subcommittee on Foreign Operations (Submitted in response to questions regarding U.S. government funding totals, purposes, and effectiveness of programming to combat trafficking in persons during Fiscal Year 2010), at 3.

[6] 2011 Department of State Report to the U.S. Senate Appropriations Committee, Subcommittee on Foreign Operations (Submitted in response to questions regarding U.S. government funding totals, purposes, and effectiveness of programming to combat trafficking in persons during Fiscal Year 2010), at 4.

becomes even more troubling in view of some of the other programs funded by the Department of State. For instance, the Economic Support Fund allocated $25.3 million for anti-trafficking purposes, but could only account for $18.6 million, while the Assistance for Europe, Eurasia, and Central Asia (AEECA) fund could only account for $6.22 out of the $9.14 million it had allocated for trafficking.[7]

In addition to the funds that simply cannot be accounted for, many of the grants awarded by the State Department appear to be duplicative. For instance, G/TIP awarded $500,000 to Catholic Relief Services and $400,000 to the International Organization for Migration, both for lobbying government officials in Chad to draft laws related to trafficking.[8] G/TIP also awarded a $178,500 grant to the International Organization for Migration to operate a case management database and another $340,000 grant to the same organization to analyze and disseminate the information in the database.[9]

Simply put, waste and duplication among international grants and among various agencies means the funds we are dedicating to this cause are not effectively combating the problems at hand. As the Government Accountability Office noted in its most recent report on human trafficking, "the U.S. government has not developed a coordinated strategy for combating trafficking abroad or developed a way to gauge results and target its overall assistance . . . thus preventing the U.S. government from determining the effectiveness of its efforts or adjusting its assistance to better meet needs."[10] Yet despite these troubling reports and statistics, S. 1301 makes no provision for increased accountability within G/TIP or any other State Department program, allowing this lack of coordination and accountability to continue unchecked. Further, S. 1301 will likely only exacerbate this problem by expanding the role of regional bureaus of the State Department without providing appropriate safeguards to ensure these bureaus are keeping track of their funding and not duplicating efforts.

Mismanagement of domestic trafficking grants

Funds allocated to fighting international human trafficking are not the only ones being mismanaged. Between April 2007 and March 2008, the DOJ Inspector General randomly audited seven trafficking grants awarded by the Justice Department and found "significant deficiencies" with all of them.[11] There are also performance problems with the task forces the Department of Justice funds around the country that coordinate state and local law enforcement

[7] 2011 Department of State Report to the U.S. Senate Appropriations Committee, Subcommittee on Foreign Operations (Submitted in response to questions regarding U.S. government funding totals, purposes, and effectiveness of programming to combat trafficking in persons during Fiscal Year 2010), at 3–5.

[8] State Department Spreadsheet of Trafficking Grants, FY2009 and FY2010 expenditures.

[9] State Department Spreadsheet of Trafficking Grants, FY2009 expenditure.

[10] GAO Report: GAO–07–915, "Human Trafficking: A Strategic Framework Could Help Enhance the Interagency Collaboration Needed to Effectively Combat Trafficking Crimes," Government Accountability Office, July 2007, *available at http://www.gao.gov/new.items/d07915.pdf*.

[11] Glenn A. Fine, "Top Management and Performance Challenges in the Department of Justice," Inspector General Memorandum, November 13, 2008, *available at http://www.justice.gov/oig/challenges/2008/index.htm*. However, in its testimony before the U.S. Senate Committee on the Judiciary on September 14, 2011, the Department of Justice asserted it had remedied the deficiencies in 6 of the 7 grants.

and federal agencies' efforts to combat trafficking. Over a four-year period there were at least 45 federally-funded task forces throughout the United States. Of the 42 task forces that reported one instance of human trafficking or more, 24 of those task forces did not provide individual-level information for at least one suspect or victim to the Department of Justice, indicating a failure of record-keeping.[12] As a result, these 24 task forces were designated "low data quality task forces" by the Office of Justice Programs, and their records were excluded from statistical reports. Thus, these tasks forces were a waste of federal resources.

S. 1301 takes some steps to alleviate these problems by including eleven accountability measures for grants awarded by the Department of Justice. However, these accountability provisions do not apply to the grants awarded by other departments and agencies. Since the authorizations for the Department of Justice in S. 1301 only account for twenty-five percent of the total authorizations, the vast majority of the funds are not affected by these provisions.

Other problematic provisions of the TVPRA

Several other problematic provisions of the TVPA remain unaddressed by S. 1301. First, there is evidence that the Department of Health and Human Services is promoting a pro-abortion agenda through its anti-trafficking grant program. A recent announcement for 2011 grant requests under the National Human Trafficking Victim Assistance Program states: "preference will be given to grantees . . . that will offer all victims referral to medical providers who can provide or refer for provision of treatment for sexually transmitted infections, family planning services and the full range of legally permissible gynecological and obstetric care. . ."[13] "Family planning services and the full range of legally permissible gynecological and obstetric care" means the grantees must be willing to refer victims to medical providers who provide abortion services. Federal agencies should not be allowed to discriminate against programs that oppose abortion and refuse to offer referrals to abortion services, yet S. 1301 takes no steps to forbid this discrimination.

Another concern stems from the amount of anti-trafficking funding that is spent on "public awareness" programs rather than victims' services, prosecutions, or prevention. While these programs may be helpful in preventing future human trafficking, there is no streamlined public awareness model being implemented around the world, which leads to higher costs and uncertainty about its effectiveness. Of the 272 grants awarded by the State Department in 2010, totaling over $108.7 million, more than one-third of them had at least a component for raising awareness of trafficking. There were 50 different grants, totaling $8.25 million, for public awareness in the United States alone.[14] Although the Department of Justice's Office of Justice Programs limits its grantees' public aware-

---

[12] Office of Justice Programs Report NCJ233732, Duren Banks and Tracey Kychelhahn, "Characteristics of Suspected Human Trafficking Incidents, 2008–2010," Bureau of Justice Statistics, Office of Justice Programs, U.S. Department of Justice, April 28, 2011, *available at http://bjs.ojp.usdoj.gov/index.cfm?ty=pbdetail&iid=2372.*

[13] U.S. Department of Health and Human Services, Administration for Children and Families website *at http://www.acf.hhs.gov/grants/open/foa/view/HHS-2011-ACF-ORR-ZV–0148.*

[14] Analysis of State Department's Spreadsheet of Trafficking Grants.

ness expenditures to 5% of the total grant, no other agency or program limits their grantees in this manner. Too much money is being spent on public awareness given the lack of demonstrable results proving this effort reduces human trafficking. These funds should instead be spent on victims' services and prosecutions of perpetrators of these crimes; once again, S. 1301 does nothing to address this concern.

Conclusion

While S. 1301 includes some improvements over previous TVPA reauthorizations, significant work remains. As mentioned previously, S. 1301 introduces an eleven-point accountability test for all Department of Justice anti-trafficking grantees; however, it fails to extend this test to any other agency's grantees. This accountability is particularly necessary for international grants under the Department of State, as their grants are especially prone to a lack of accountability.

Further, S. 1301 reduces authorizations for anti-trafficking programs to $130 million, which is $10 million below the amount appropriated in FY2010. While this reduction is admirable, it simply does not go far enough in light of the economic climate and our national debt. The federal government could spend far less on anti-trafficking programs, while simultaneously achieving greater success, simply by eliminating wasteful and duplicative programs. Finally, as the majority notes in its views, additional funding to combat human trafficking is being provided to these departments and agencies through other appropriations bills; thus, reducing authorizations in this bill will likely result in departments and agencies directing their energies to seeking additional funds from other sources rather than forcing them to better manage the funds they receive.

Our national debt now exceeds $14 trillion; therefore, we must ensure that our tax dollars are responsibly spent even on the most important areas. Taxpayers expect us to work together to reduce wasteful and unnecessary spending and be more vigilant about how we spend public funds. Before we pass the Trafficking Victims Protection Reauthorization Act, Congress must ensure our resources are actually combating human trafficking and not being wasted or mismanaged. Unfortunately, the bill as currently written fails to address these issues. Absent significant amendments to correct the problems highlighted, the Senate should reject S. 1301 and work towards crafting a more effective and efficient Trafficking Victims Protection Act.

JON KYL.
JEFF SESSIONS.
MICHAEL S. LEE.
TOM COBURN.

MINORITY VIEWS FROM SENATORS CORNYN AND KYL

Every year, an estimated 100,000 American juveniles are victimized through domestic child prostitution.[1] In addressing the problem of human trafficking, the sex trafficking of children in the United States should be the government's first priority. S. 1301, however, contains inadequate funding, protections, and law enforcement tools to meet this challenge. The Cornyn/Kyl amendment (ALB 11813) would add the full text of the Domestic Minor Sex Trafficking Deterrence and Victims Support Act (S. 596) to S. 1301, taking a more comprehensive approach to fighting the evils of domestic sex trafficking through both victims' services and law enforcement tools. S. 1301 should not be passed by the Senate without including the language of ALB11813.

Enhanced and targeted grant programs to combat domestic minor sex trafficking

S. 1301 authorizes $8 million per year to be distributed through 4 block grants to state and local governments in order to combat the sex trafficking of minors in the United States. ALB11813 would authorize $14 million for six such block grants, and would require grantees to certify that these funds would only be allocated to serve interstate victims of sex trafficking. The enhanced and targeted grants under ALB11813 would make greater strides in developing a best practices model for nationwide sex trafficking deterrence and would ensure that these funds are directed toward fulfilling the federal government's interstate role in protecting children in the United States from sex traffickers. Additionally, ALB11813 would provide for greater grantee accountability by enacting a 25% grantee match requirement in the first year of the grant. S. 1301 only requires a 15% grantee match during the same period.

Comprehensive law enforcement tools to deter domestic minor sex trafficking

Under S. 1301, block grants to state and local governments to combat the sex trafficking of minors could be used to provide: residential care, emergency social services, daily necessities, case management services, mental health counseling, legal services, and referral services for minor victims of sex trafficking, as well as specialized training for personnel likely to encounter sex trafficking victims and education programs to provide information about the prevention of sex trafficking. ALB11813 would add an enhanced law enforcement component to these authorized uses, including: specialized anti-trafficking training for law enforcement personnel, salaries for law enforcement personnel engaged in trafficking deter-

---

[1] Shared Hope International. "National Report on Domestic Minor Sex Trafficking". p.4. 2009.

rence, investigation expenses for cases involving the sex trafficking of minors, and salaries for prosecutors in sex trafficking cases.

ALB11813 would also grant administrative subpoena power to the U.S. Marshals Service for the sole purpose of investigating unregistered sex offenders. According to the Marshals Service, there are currently more than 100,000 unregistered sex offenders living in the United States.[2] These sex offenders pose a high risk of engaging in illicit sexual conduct,[3] and are often very difficult to track down—moving from place-to-place and traveling under aliases in order to conceal their location and identity.[4] Investigations of fugitive sex offenders therefore repeatedly involve a long and complicated paper trail. This very narrow provision would allow the U.S. Marshals service to investigate these offenders more effectively by quickly seizing items such as rent records and credit card accounts.

ALB11813 would also impose a 1-year federal mandatory minimum sentence for the possession of child pornography depicting a pre-pubescent minor younger than the age of 12. Additionally, it would increase the maximum federal sentence for the possession of such pornography from 10 to 20 years. Many of the children depicted in this form of pornography are actually victims of human trafficking,[5] and criminals who possess this material pose a heightened risk to engage in sexual behavior with children.[6] All too often, however, we have seen federal judges downward depart and hand out lenient sentences for this crime.[7] This provision would send a strong message to child pornographers and traffickers, while providing law enforcement with a valuable tool to deter and punish behavior that directly aids and abets human trafficking.

Protections for children who confront human traffickers in court

ALB11813 would provide protections for child witnesses who choose to cooperate with law enforcement investigations by confronting their traffickers in a court of law. The amendment would add language to 18 U.S.C. 1514 requiring a federal court to issue a protective order prohibiting the harassment or intimidation of a minor victim or witness if the court finds evidence that the conduct at issue is reasonable likely to adversely affect the willingness of the minor victim or witness to testify or otherwise participate in the federal criminal case or investigation. ALB11813 would also provide penalties of up to 5 years in prison for the knowing and intentional violation of a child witness protective order. These provisions would provide strong protections for child witnesses where

[2] Hylton, Stacia. "Statement of Stacia Hylton Before the House Judiciary Subcommittee on Crime, Terrorism, and Homeland Security:The Reauthorization of the Adam Walsh Act". p.1. 15 FEB 2011.

[3] Karl Hanson, Kelly Morton and Andrew Harris. "Sexual Offender Recidivism Risk: What We Know and What We Need to Know. Annals of the New York Academy of Sciences, volume 989. pp. 154–166. 2003.

[4] Wolf, Isaac. "Many Sex Offenders Disappear". Scripps Howard News Service. 7 NOV 2010.

[5] Hughes, Donna. "The Demand for Victims of Sex Trafficking." University of Rhode Island. p.26. 2005.

[6] Michael Bourke and Andres Hernandez. "The Butner Study' Redux: A Report on the Incidence of Hands-on Child Victimization by Child Pornography Offenders. Journal of Family Violence. Vol. 24, No. 3. pp. 183–191. 2009.

[7] United States Sentencing Commission. "The History of the Child Pornography Guidelines". p.11. 2009.

the attorney of a sex trafficker seeks to intimidate and discourage the testimony of that witness. Because child witnesses are often asked to testify against an alleged sex trafficker, this provision would help to ensure that these traffickers are punished to the full extent of the law.[8]

A bipartisan piece of legislation

ALB11813 is substantially identical to both S. 2925 (111th Congress) and S. 596 (112th Congress). S. 2925 passed the Senate Judiciary Committee unanimously on August 5th, 2010, and proceeded to pass the full Senate by unanimous consent on December 9th, 2010. The bill was sponsored by Senator Wyden, and co-sponsored by four members of the Judiciary Committee: Senators Cornyn, Durbin, Franken and Schumer. S. 596 was introduced on March 16, 2011 by Senator Wyden and co-sponsored by five members of the Judiciary Committee: Senators Cornyn, Kyl, Blumenthal, Klobuchar and Schumer.

Conclusion

The interstate sex trafficking of children in the United States should be the top priority of the federal government in attempting to combat human trafficking. S. 1301, in its current form, contains insufficient law enforcement tools and resources to fulfill this responsibility. Though ALB 11813 is not, itself, sufficient to remedy the evils of domestic minor sex trafficking, it is a substantial step in the right direction. The Senate should not pass S. 1301 without, at the very least, including the language of ALB11813.

JOHN CORNYN.
JON KYL.

---

[8] United Nations Office of Drugs and Crime. "Toolkit to Combat Trafficking in Persons". 258–260. 2008.

VIII. Changes to Existing Law Made by the Bill, as Reported

In compliance with paragraph 12 of rule XXVI of the Standing Rules of the Senate, changes in existing law made by S. 1301, as reported, are shown as follows (existing law proposed to be omitted is enclosed in black brackets, new matter is printed in italic, and existing law in which no change is proposed is shown in roman):

UNITED STATES CODE

TITLE 8—ALIENS AND NATIONALITY

* * * * * * *

CHAPTER 12—IMMIGRATION AND NATIONALITY

* * * * * * *

SEC. 1101. DEFINITIONS.
(a) As used in this chapter.—

* * * * * * *

(15) The term "immigrant" means every alien except an alien who is within one of the following classes of nonimmigrant aliens—

* * * * * * *

(T)(i) subject to section 1184(o) of this title, an alien who the Secretary of Homeland Security, or in the case of subclause (III)(aa) the Secretary of Homeland Security, in consultation with the Attorney General, determines—

(I) is or has been a victim of a severe form of trafficking in persons, as defined in section 7102 of Title 22;

(II) is physically present in the United States, American Samoa, or the Commonwealth of the Northern Mariana Islands, or at a port of entry thereto, on account of such trafficking, including physical presence on account of the alien having been allowed entry into the United States for participation in investigative or judicial processes associated with an act or a perpetrator of trafficking;

(III)(aa) has complied with any reasonable request for assistance in the Federal, State, or local investigation or prosecution of acts of trafficking or the investigation of crime where acts of trafficking are at least one central reason for the commission of that crime;

(bb) in consultation with the Attorney General, as appropriate, is unable to cooperate with a request described in item (aa) due to physical or psychological trauma; or

(cc) has not attained 18 years of age; and

(IV) the alien would suffer extreme hardship involving unusual and severe harm upon removal; and

(ii) if accompanying, or following to join, the alien described in clause (i)—

(I) in the case of an alien described in clause (i) who is under 21 years of age, the spouse, children, unmarried siblings under 18 years of age on the date on which such alien applied for status under such clause, and parents of such alien;

(II) in the case of an alien described in clause (i) who is 21 years of age or older, the spouse and children of such alien; or

(III) any parent or unmarried sibling under 18 years of age, *or any adult or minor children of a derivative beneficiary of the alien, as* of an alien described in subclause (I) or (II) who the Secretary of Homeland Security, in consultation with the law enforcement officer investigating a severe form of trafficking, determines faces a present danger of retaliation as a result of the alien's escape from the severe form of trafficking or cooperation with law enforcement.

(iii) Repealed. Pub. L. 110–457, Title II, § 201(a)(3), Dec. 23, 2008, 122 Stat. 5053

(U)(i) subject to section 1184(p) of this title, an alien who files a petition for status under this subparagraph, if the Secretary of Homeland Security determines that—

(I) the alien has suffered substantial physical or mental abuse as a result of having been a victim of criminal activity described in clause (iii);

(II) the alien (or in the case of an alien child under the age of 16, the parent, guardian, or next friend of the alien) possesses information concerning criminal activity described in clause (iii);

(III) the alien (or in the case of an alien child under the age of 16, the parent, guardian, or next friend of the alien) has been helpful, is being helpful, or is likely to be helpful to a Federal, State, or local law enforcement official, to a Federal, State, or local prosecutor, to a Federal or State judge, to the Service, or to other Federal, State, or local authorities investigating or prosecuting criminal activity described in clause (iii); and

(IV) the criminal activity described in clause (iii) violated the laws of the United States or occurred in the United States (including in Indian country and military installations) or the territories and possessions of the United States;

(ii) if accompanying, or following to join, the alien described in clause (i)—

(I) in the case of an alien described in clause (i) who is under 21 years of age, the spouse, children, unmarried siblings under 18 years of age on the date on which such alien applied for status under such clause, and parents of such alien; or

(II) in the case of an alien described in clause (i) who is 21 years of age or older, the spouse and children of such alien; and

(iii) the criminal activity referred to in this clause is that involving one or more of the following or any similar activity in violation of Federal, State, or local criminal law: rape; torture; trafficking; incest; domestic violence; sexual assault; abusive sexual contact; prostitution; sexual exploitation; female genital mutilation; being held hostage; peonage; involuntary servitude; slave trade; kidnapping; abduction; unlawful criminal restraint; false imprisonment; blackmail; extortion; manslaughter; murder; felonious assault; witness tampering; obstruction of justice; perjury; *fraud in foreign labor contracting (as defined in section 1351 of title 18, United States Code);* or attempt, conspiracy, or solicitation to commit any of the above mentioned crimes; or

*　　*　　*　　*　　*　　*　　*

SEC. 1232. ENHANCING EFFORTS TO COMBAT THE TRAFFICKING OF CHILDREN.

*　　*　　*　　*　　*　　*　　*

(c) PROVIDING SAFE AND SECURE PLACEMENTS FOR CHILDREN.—

(1) POLICIES AND PROGRAMS.—The Secretary of Health and Human Services, Secretary of Homeland Security, Attorney General, and Secretary of State shall establish policies and programs to ensure that unaccompanied alien children in the United States are protected from traffickers and other persons seeking to victimize or otherwise engage such children in criminal, harmful, or exploitative activity, including policies and programs reflecting best practices in witness security programs.

(2) SAFE AND SECURE PLACEMENTS.—

[Subject to] *(A) MINORS IN DEPARTMENT OF HEALTH AND HUMAN SERVICES CUSTODY.—Subject to* section 279(b)(2) of Title 6, an unaccompanied alien child in the custody of the Secretary of Health and Human Services shall be promptly placed in the least restrictive setting that is in the best interest of the child. In making such placements, the Secretary may consider danger to self, danger to the community, and risk of flight. Placement of child trafficking victims may include placement in an Unaccompanied Refugee Minor program, pursuant to section 412(d) of the Immigration and Nationality Act (8 U.S.C. § 1522(d)), if a suitable family member is not available to provide care. A child shall not be placed in a secure facility absent a determination that the child poses a danger to self or others or has been charged with having committed a criminal offense. The placement of a child in a secure facility shall be reviewed, at a minimum, on a monthly basis, in accordance with procedures prescribed by the Secretary, to determine if such placement remains warranted.

(B) ALIENS TRANSFERRED FROM DEPARTMENT OF HEALTH AND HUMAN SERVICES TO DEPARTMENT OF HOMELAND SECURITY CUSTODY.—If a minor described in subparagraph (A) reaches 18 years of age and is transferred to the custody of the Secretary of Homeland Security, the Secretary shall

consider placement in the least restrictive setting available after taking into account the alien's danger to self, danger to the community, and risk of flight. Such aliens shall be eligible to participate in alternative to detention programs, utilizing a continuum of alternatives based on the alien's need for supervision, which may include placement of the alien with an individual or an organizational sponsor, or in a supervised group home.

(3) SAFETY AND SUITABILITY ASSESSMENTS.—

(A) IN GENERAL.—Subject to the requirements of subparagraph (B), an unaccompanied alien child may not be placed with a person or entity unless the Secretary of Health and Human Services makes a determination that the proposed custodian is capable of providing for the child's physical and mental well-being. Such determination shall, at a minimum, include verification of the custodian's identity and relationship to the child, if any, as well as an independent finding that the individual has not engaged in any activity that would indicate a potential risk to the child.

(B) HOME STUDIES.—Before placing the child with an individual, the Secretary of Health and Human Services shall determine whether a home study is first necessary. A home study shall be conducted for a child who is a victim of a severe form of trafficking in persons, a special needs child with a disability (as defined in section 12102(2) of Title 42), a child who has been a victim of physical or sexual abuse under circumstances that indicate that the child's health or welfare has been significantly harmed or threatened, or a child whose proposed sponsor clearly presents a risk of abuse, maltreatment, exploitation, or trafficking to the child based on all available objective evidence. The Secretary of Health and Human Services shall conduct follow-up services, during the pendency of removal proceedings, on children for whom a home study was conducted and is authorized to conduct follow-up services in cases involving children with mental health or other needs who could benefit from ongoing assistance from a social welfare agency.

(C) ACCESS TO INFORMATION.—Not later than 2 weeks after receiving a request from the Secretary of Health and Human Services, the Secretary of Homeland Security shall provide information necessary to conduct suitability assessments from appropriate Federal, State, and local law enforcement and immigration databases.

(4) LEGAL ORIENTATION PRESENTATIONS.—The Secretary of Health and Human Services shall cooperate with the Executive Office for Immigration Review to ensure that custodians receive legal orientation presentations provided through the Legal Orientation Program administered by the Executive Office for Immigration Review. At a minimum, such presentations shall address the custodian's responsibility to attempt to ensure the child's appearance at all immigration proceedings

and to protect the child from mistreatment, exploitation, and trafficking.

(5) ACCESS TO COUNSEL.—The Secretary of Health and Human Services shall ensure, to the greatest extent practicable and consistent with section 292 of the Immigration and Nationality Act (8 U.S.C. 1362), that all unaccompanied alien children who are or have been in the custody of the Secretary or the Secretary of Homeland Security, and who are not described in subsection (a)(2)(A), have counsel to represent them in legal proceedings or matters and protect them from mistreatment, exploitation, and trafficking. To the greatest extent practicable, the Secretary of Health and Human Services shall make every effort to utilize the services of pro bono counsel who agree to provide representation to such children without charge.

(6) CHILD ADVOCATES.—

[The Secretary] *(A) IN GENERAL.—The Secretary* of Health and Human Services is authorized to appoint independent child advocates for child trafficking victims and other vulnerable unaccompanied alien children. A child advocate shall be provided access to materials necessary to effectively advocate for the best interest of the child. The child advocate shall not be compelled to testify or provide evidence in any proceeding concerning any information or opinion received from the child in the course of serving as a child advocate. The child advocate shall be presumed to be acting in good faith and be immune from civil [and criminal] liability for lawful conduct of duties as described in this provision.

(B) APPOINTMENT OF CHILD ADVOCATES.—

(i) INITIAL SITES.—Not later than 2 years after the date of the enactment of the Trafficking Victims Protection Reauthorization Act of 2011, the Secretary of Health and Human Services shall appoint child advocates at 3 new immigration detention sites to provide independent child advocates for trafficking victims and vulnerable unaccompanied alien children.

(ii) ADDITIONAL SITES.—Not later than 3 years after the date of the enactment of the Trafficking Victims Protection Reauthorization Act of 2011, the Secretary shall appoint child advocates at not more than 3 additional immigration detention sites.

(iii) SELECTION OF SITES.—Sites at which child advocate programs will be established under this subparagraph shall be located at immigration detention sites at which more than 50 children are held in immigration custody, and shall be selected sequentially, with priority given to locations with—

(I) the largest number of unaccompanied alien children; and

(II) the most vulnerable populations of unaccompanied children.

(C) RESTRICTIONS.—

(i) ADMINISTRATIVE EXPENSES.—A child advocate program may not use more that 10 percent of the Federal funds received under this section for administrative expenses.

(ii) NONEXCLUSIVITY.—Nothing in this section may be construed to restrict the ability of a child advocate program under this section to apply for or obtain funding from any other source to carry out the programs described in this section.

(iii) CONTRIBUTION OF FUNDS.—A child advocate program selected under this section shall contribute non-Federal funds, either directly or through in-kind contributions, to the costs of the child advocate program in an amount that is not less than 25 percent of the total amount of Federal funds received by the child advocate program under this section. In-kind contributions may not exceed 40 percent of the matching requirement under this clause.

(D) ANNUAL REPORT TO CONGRESS.—Not later than 1 year after the date of the enactment of the Trafficking Victims Protection Reauthorization Act of 2011, and annually thereafter, the Secretary of Health and Human Services shall submit a report describing the activities undertaken by the Secretary to authorize the appointment of independent Child Advocates for trafficking victims and vulnerable unaccompanied alien children to the Committee on the Judiciary of the Senate and the Committee on the Judiciary of the House of Representatives.

(E) ASSESSMENT OF CHILD ADVOCATE PROGRAM.—

(i) IN GENERAL.—As soon as practicable after the date of the enactment of the Trafficking Victims Protection Reauthorization Act of 2011, the Comptroller General of the United States shall conduct a study regarding the effectiveness of the Child Advocate Program operated by the Secretary of Health and Human Services.

(ii) MATTERS TO BE STUDIED.—In the study required under clause (i), the Comptroller General shall—

(I) analyze the effectiveness of existing child advocate programs in improving outcomes for trafficking victims and other vulnerable unaccompanied alien children;

(II) evaluate the implementation of child advocate programs in new sites pursuant to subparagraph (B);

(III) evaluate the extent to which eligible trafficking victims and other vulnerable unaccompanied children are receiving child advocate services and assess the possible budgetary implications of increased participation in the program;

(IV) evaluate the barriers to improving outcomes for trafficking victims and other vulnerable unaccompanied children; and

(V) make recommendations on statutory changes to improve the Child Advocate Program in relation *to the matters analyzed under subclauses (I) through (IV).*

(iii) GAO REPORT.—Not later than 3 years after the date of the enactment of this Act, the Comptroller General of the United States shall submit the results of the study required under this subparagraph to—

(I) the Committee on the Judiciary of the Senate;

(II) the Committee on Health, Education, Labor, and Pensions of the Senate;

(III) the Committee on the Judiciary of the House of Representatives; and (IV) the Committee on Education and the Workforce of the House of Representatives.

(F) AUTHORIZATION OF APPROPRIATIONS.—There are authorized to be appropriated to the Secretary and Human Services to carry out this subsection—

(i) $1,000,000 for each of the fiscal years 2012 and 2013; and

(ii) $2,000,000 for each of the fiscal years 2014 and 2015.

(d) PERMANENT PROTECTION FOR CERTAIN AT-RISK CHILDREN.—

(1) Omitted

(2) EXPEDITIOUS ADJUDICATION.—All applications for special immigrant status under section 101(a)(27)(J) of the Immigration and Nationality Act (8 U.S.C. 1101(a)(27)(J)) shall be adjudicated by the Secretary of Homeland Security not later than 180 days after the date on which the application is filed.

(3) Omitted

(4) ELIGIBILITY FOR ASSISTANCE.—

(A) IN GENERAL.—A child who has been granted special immigrant status under section 101(a)(27)(J) of the Immigration and Nationality Act (8 U.S.C. 1101(a)(27)(J)) and who was [either] in the custody of the Secretary of Health and Human Services at the time a dependency order was granted for such child [or who], was receiving services pursuant to section 501(a) of the Refugee Education Assistance Act of 1980 (8 U.S.C. 1522 note) at the time such dependency order was granted, *or has been granted status under section 101(a)(15)(U) of the Immigration and Nationality Act (8 U.S.C. 1101(a)(15)(U)),* shall be eligible for placement and services under section 412(d) of the Immigration and Nationality Act (8 U.S.C. 1522(d)) until the earlier of—

(i) the date on which the child reaches the age designated in section 412(d)(2)(B) of the Immigration and Nationality Act (8 U.S.C. 1522(d)(2)(B)); or

(ii) the date on which the child is placed in a permanent adoptive home.

(B) STATE REIMBURSEMENT.—Subject to the availability of appropriations, if State foster care funds are expended on behalf of a child who is not described in subparagraph (A) and has been granted special immigrant status under section 101(a)(27)(J) of the Immigration and Nationality Act (8 U.S.C. 1101(a)(27)(J)), *or status under section*

101(a)(15)(U) of the Immigration and Nationality Act (8 U.S.C. 1101(a)(15)(U)), the Federal Government shall reimburse the State in which the child resides for such expenditures by the State.

(5) STATE COURTS ACTING IN LOCO PARENTIS.—A department or agency of a State, or an individual or entity appointed by a State court or juvenile court located in the United States, acting in loco parentis, shall not be considered a legal guardian for purposes of this section or section 279 of Title 6.

(6) TRANSITION RULE.—Notwithstanding any other provision of law, an alien described in section 101(a)(27)(J) of the Immigration and Nationality Act (8 U.S.C. 1101(a)(27)(J)), as amended by paragraph (1), may not be denied special immigrant status under such section after December 23, 2008 based on age if the alien was a child on the date on which the alien applied for such status.

(7) Omitted

(8) SPECIALIZED NEEDS OF UNACCOMPANIED ALIEN CHILDREN.—Applications for asylum and other forms of relief from removal in which an unaccompanied alien child is the principal applicant shall be governed by regulations which take into account the specialized needs of unaccompanied alien children and which address both procedural and substantive aspects of handling unaccompanied alien children's cases.

*   *   *   *   *   *   *

SEC. 1375b. PROTECTIONS FOR DOMESTIC WORKERS AND OTHER NONIMMIGRANTS.

(a) INFORMATION PAMPHLET *AND VIDEO FOR CONSULAR WAITING ROOMS.*—

(1) DEVELOPMENT AND DISTRIBUTION.—The Secretary of State, in consultation with the Secretary of Homeland Security, the Attorney General, and the Secretary of Labor, shall develop an information pamphlet *and video* on legal rights and resources for aliens applying for employment- or education-based nonimmigrant visas. *The video shall be distributed and shown in consular waiting rooms in embassies and consulates determined to have the greatest concentration of employment or education-based non-immigrant visa applicants, and where sufficient video facilities exist in waiting or other rooms where applicants wait or convene. The Secretary of State is authorized to augment video facilities in such consulates or embassies in order to fulfill the purposes of this section.*

(2) CONSULTATION.—In developing the information pamphlet under paragraph (1), the Secretary of State shall consult with nongovernmental organizations with expertise on the legal rights of workers and victims of severe forms of trafficking in persons.

(b) CONTENTS.—The information pamphlet *and video* developed under subsection (a) shall include information concerning items such as—

(1) the nonimmigrant visa application processes, including information about the portability of employment;

(2) the legal rights of employment or education-based non-immigrant visa holders under Federal immigration, labor, and employment law;

(3) the illegality of slavery, peonage, trafficking in persons, sexual assault, extortion, blackmail, and worker exploitation in the United States;

(4) the legal rights of immigrant victims of trafficking in persons and worker exploitation, including—

(A) the right of access to immigrant and labor rights groups;

(B) the right to seek redress in United States courts;

(C) the right to report abuse without retaliation;

(D) the right of the nonimmigrant to relinquish possession of his or her passport to his or her employer;

(E) the requirement of an employment contract between the employer and the nonimmigrant; and

(F) an explanation of the rights and protections included in the contract described in subparagraph (E); and

(5) information about nongovernmental organizations that provide services for victims of trafficking in persons and worker exploitation, including—

(A) anti-trafficking in persons telephone hotlines operated by the Federal Government;

(B) the Operation Rescue and Restore hotline; and

(C) a general description of the types of victims services available for individuals subject to trafficking in persons or worker exploitation.

(c) TRANSLATION.—

(1) IN GENERAL.—To best serve the language groups having the greatest concentration of employment-based nonimmigrant visas, the Secretary of State shall translate the information pamphlet *and produce or dub the video* developed under subsection (a) into all relevant foreign languages, to be determined by the Secretary based on the languages spoken by the greatest concentrations of employment- or education-based nonimmigrant visa applicants.

(2) REVISION.—Every 2 years, the Secretary of State, in consultation with the Attorney General and the Secretary of Homeland Security, shall determine the specific languages into which the information pamphlet will be translated *and the video produced or dubbed* based on the languages spoken by the greatest concentrations of employment- or education-based nonimmigrant visa applicants.

(d) AVAILABILITY AND DISTRIBUTION.—

(1) POSTING ON FEDERAL WEBSITES.—The information pamphlet *and video* developed under subsection (a) shall be posted on the websites of the Department of State, the Department of Homeland Security, the Department of Justice, the Department of Labor, and all United States consular posts processing applications for employment- or education-based nonimmigrant visas.

(2) OTHER DISTRIBUTION.—The information pamphlet *and video* developed under subsection (a) shall be made available to any—

(A) government agency;

(B) nongovernmental advocacy organization; or

(C) foreign labor broker doing business in the United States.

(3) DEADLINE FOR PAMPHLET DEVELOPMENT AND DISTRIBU-TION.—Not later than 180 days after December 23, 2008, the Secretary of State shall distribute and make available the information pamphlet developed under subsection (a) in all the languages referred to in subsection (c).

(4) DEADLINE FOR VIDEO DEVELOPMENT AND DISTRIBUTION.—Not later than 1 year after the date of the enactment of the Trafficking Victims Protection Reauthorization Act of 2011, the Secretary of State shall make available the video developed under subsection (a) produced or dubbed in all the languages referred to in subsection (c).

*　　*　　*　　*　　*　　*　　*

TITLE 18—CRIMES AND CRIMINAL PROCEDURE

*　　*　　*　　*　　*　　*　　*

PART I—CRIMES

*　　*　　*　　*　　*　　*　　*

CHAPTER 77—PEONAGE, SLAVERY, AND TRAFFICKING IN PERSONS

*　　*　　*　　*　　*　　*　　*

TABLE OF CONTENTS.

*　　*　　*　　*　　*　　*　　*

SEC. 1597. UNLAWFUL CONDUCT WITH RESPECT TO IMMIGRATION DOCUMENTS.

(a) DESTRUCTION, CONCEALMENT, REMOVAL, CONFISCATION, OR POSSESSION OF IMMIGRATION DOCUMENTS.—It shall be unlawful for any person to knowingly destroy, conceal, remove, confiscate, or possess, an actual or purported passport or other immigration document of another individual—

(1) in the course of violating section 1351 of this title or section 274 of the Immigration and Nationality Act (8 U.S.C. 1324);

(2) with intent to violate section 1351 of this title or section 274 of the Immigration and Nationality Act (8 U.S.C. 1324); or

(3) in order to, without lawful authority, maintain, prevent, or restrict the labor of services of the individual.

(b) PENALTY.—Any person who violates subsection (a) shall be fined under this title, imprisoned for not more than 1 year, or both.

(c) OBSTRUCTION.—Any person who knowingly obstructs, attempts to obstruct, or in any way interferes with or prevents the enforcement of this section, shall be subject to the penalties described in subsection (b).

*　　*　　*　　*　　*　　*　　*

CHAPTER 96—RACKETEER INFLUENCED AND CORRUPT ORGANIZATIONS

*　　*　　*　　*　　*　　*　　*

SEC. 1961. DEFINITIONS.

As used in this chapter—

(1) "racketeering activity" means—

(A) any act or threat involving murder, kidnapping, gambling, arson, robbery, bribery, extortion, dealing in obscene matter, or dealing in a controlled substance or listed chemical (as defined in section 102 of the Controlled Substances Act), which is chargeable under State law and punishable by imprisonment for more than one year;

(B) any act which is indictable under any of the following provisions of title 18, United States Code: Section 201 (relating to bribery), section 224 (relating to sports bribery), sections 471, 472, and 473 (relating to counterfeiting), section 659 (relating to theft from interstate shipment) if the act indictable under section 659 is felonious, section 664 (relating to embezzlement from pension and welfare funds), sections 891–894 (relating to extortionate credit transactions), section 1028 (relating to fraud and related activity in connection with identification documents), section 1029 (relating to fraud and related activity in connection with access devices), section 1084 (relating to the transmission of gambling information), section 1341 (relating to mail fraud), section 1343 (relating to wire fraud), section 1344 (relating to financial institution fraud), *section 1351 (relating to fraud in foreign labor contracting)*, section 1425 (relating to the procurement of citizenship or nationalization unlawfully), section 1426 (relating to the reproduction of naturalization or citizenship papers), section 1427 (relating to the sale of naturalization or citizenship papers), sections 1461–1465 (relating to obscene matter), section 1503 (relating to obstruction of justice), section 1510 (relating to obstruction of criminal investigations), section 1511 (relating to the obstruction of State or local law enforcement), section 1512 (relating to tampering with a witness, victim, or an informant), section 1513 (relating to retaliating against a witness, victim, or an informant), section 1542 (relating to false statement in application and use of passport), section 1543 (relating to forgery or false use of passport), section 1544 (relating to misuse of passport), section 1546 (relating to fraud and misuse of visas, permits, and other documents), sections 1581–1592 (relating to peonage, slavery, and trafficking in persons), section 1951 (relating to interference with commerce, robbery, or extortion), section 1952 (relating to racketeering), section 1953 (relating to interstate transportation of wagering paraphernalia), section 1954 (relating to unlawful welfare fund payments), section 1955 (relating to the prohibition of illegal gambling businesses), section 1956 (relating to the laundering of monetary instruments), section 1957 (relating to engaging in monetary transactions in property derived from specified unlawful activity), section 1958 (relating to use of interstate commerce facilities in the commission of murder-for-hire), section 1960 (relating to illegal money transmitters), sections 2251, 2251A, 2252, and 2260 (relating to sexual exploitation of children), sections 2312 and 2313 (relating to interstate transportation of stolen motor vehicles), sections 2314 and 2315 (relating to interstate transportation of stolen property), section 2318 (relating to trafficking in counterfeit labels for phonorecords, computer programs or computer program documentation or packaging and copies of motion pictures or other audiovisual works), section 2319 (relating to criminal infringement of a copyright), section 2319A (relating to unauthorized fixation of and trafficking in sound recordings and music videos of live musical performances), section 2320 (relating to trafficking in goods or services bearing counterfeit marks), section 2321 (relating to trafficking in certain motor vehicles or motor vehicle parts), sections 2341–2346 (relating to trafficking in contraband cigarettes), sections 2421–24 (relating to white slave traffic), sections 175–178 (relating to biological weapons), sections 229–229F (relating to chemical weapons), section 831 (relating to nuclear materials),

(C) any act which is indictable under title 29, United States Code, section 186 (dealing with restrictions on payments and loans to labor organizations) or section 501(c) (relating to embezzlement from union funds),

(D) any offense involving fraud connected with a case under title 11 (except a case under section 157 of this title), fraud in the sale of securities, or the felonious manufacture, importation, receiving, concealment, buying, selling, or otherwise dealing in a controlled substance or listed chemical (as defined in section 102 of the Controlled Substances Act), punishable under any law of the United States, (E) any act which is indictable under the Currency and Foreign Transactions Reporting Act, (F) any act which is indictable under the Immigration and Nationality Act, section 274 (relating to bringing in and harboring certain aliens), section 277 (relating to aiding or assisting certain aliens to enter the United States), or section 278 (relating to importation of alien for immoral purpose) if the act indictable under such section of such Act was committed for the purpose of financial gain, or (G) any act that is indictable under any provision listed in section 2332b(g)(5)(B);

* * * * * * *

CHAPTER 110—SEXUAL EXPLOITATION AND OTHER ABUSE OF CHILDREN

* * * * * * *

SEC. 2255. CIVIL REMEDY FOR PERSONAL INJURIES.

(a) IN GENERAL.—Any person who, while a minor, was a victim of a violation of [section 2241(c)] *section 1589, 1590, 1591, 2241(c),* 2242, 2243, 2251, 2251A, 2252, 2252A, 2260, 2421, 2422, or 2423 of this title and who suffers personal injury as a result of such violation, regardless of whether the injury occurred while such person was a minor, may sue in any appropriate United States District Court and shall recover the actual damages such person sustains and the cost of the suit, including a reasonable attorney's fee. Any person as described in the preceding sentence shall be deemed to have sustained damages of no less than $150,000 in value.

(b) STATUTE OF LIMITATIONS.—Any action commenced under this section shall be barred unless the complaint is filed within [six years] *10 years* after the right of action first accrues or in the case of a person under a legal disability, not later than three years after the disability.

* * * * * * *

CHAPTER 117—TRANSPORTATION FOR ILLEGAL SEXUAL ACTIVITIES AND RELATED CRIMES

* * * * * * *

SEC. 2423. TRANSPORTATION OF MINORS.

(a) TRANSPORTATION WITH INTENT TO ENGAGE IN CRIMINAL SEXUAL ACTIVITY.—A person who knowingly transports an individual who has not attained the age of 18 years in interstate or foreign commerce, or in any commonwealth, territory or possession of the United States, with intent that the individual engage in prostitution, or in any sexual activity for which any person can be charged with a criminal offense, shall be fined under this title and imprisoned not less than 10 years or for life.

(b) TRAVEL WITH INTENT TO ENGAGE IN ILLICIT SEXUAL CONDUCT.—A person who travels in interstate commerce or travels into the United States, or a United States citizen or an alien admitted for permanent residence in the United States who travels in foreign commerce, for the purpose of engaging in any illicit sexual conduct with another person shall be fined under this title or imprisoned not more than 30 years, or both.

(c) ENGAGING IN ILLICIT SEXUAL CONDUCT IN FOREIGN PLACES.— Any United States citizen or alien admitted for permanent residence who travels in foreign commerce *or resides, either temporarily or permanently, in a foreign country,* and engages in any illicit sexual conduct with another person shall be fined under this title or imprisoned not more than 30 years, or both.

(d) ANCILLARY OFFENSES.—Whoever, for the purpose of commercial advantage or private financial gain, arranges, induces, procures, or facilitates the travel of a person knowing that such a person is traveling in interstate commerce or foreign commerce for the purpose of engaging in illicit sexual conduct shall be fined under this title, imprisoned not more than 30 years, or both.

(e) ATTEMPT AND CONSPIRACY.—Whoever attempts or conspires to violate subsection (a), (b), (c), or (d) shall be punishable in the same manner as a completed violation of that subsection.

(f) DEFINITION.—As used in this section, the term "illicit sexual conduct" means (1) a sexual act (as defined in section 2246) with a person under 18 years of age that would be in violation of chapter 109A if the sexual act occurred in the special maritime and territorial jurisdiction of the United States; or (2) any commercial sex act (as defined in section 1591) with a person under 18 years of age.

(g) DEFENSE.—In a prosecution under this section based on illicit sexual conduct as defined in subsection (f)(2), it is a defense, which the defendant must establish by a preponderance of the evidence, that the defendant reasonably believed that the person with whom the defendant engaged in the commercial sex act had attained the age of 18 years.

* * * * * * *

TITLE 22—FOREIGN RELATIONS AND INTERCOURSE

* * * * * * *

CHAPTER 32—FOREIGN ASSISTANCE

* * * * * * *

SEC. 2151n. HUMAN RIGHTS AND DEVELOPMENT ASSISTANCE.

* * * * * * *

(g) CHILD MARRIAGE STATUS.—

(1) IN GENERAL.—The report required under subsection (d) shall include, for each country in which child marriage is prevalent, a description of the status of the practice of child marriage in such country.

(2) DEFINED TERM.—In this subsection, the term "child marriage" means the marriage of a girl or boy who is—

(A) younger than the minimum age for marriage under the laws of the country in which such girl or boy is a resident; or

(B) younger than 18 years of age, if no such law exists.

*   *   *   *   *   *   *

SEC. 2304. HUMAN RIGHTS AND SECURITY ASSISTANCE.

*   *   *   *   *   *   *

(i) CHILD MARRIAGE STATUS.—

(1) IN GENERAL.—The report required under subsection (b) shall include, for each country in which child marriage is prevalent, a description of the status of the practice of child marriage in such country.

(2) DEFINED TERM.—In this subsection, the term 'child marriage' means the marriage of a girl or boy who is—

(A) younger than the minimum age for marriage under the laws of the country in which such girl or boy is a resident; or

(B) younger than 18 years of age, if no such law exists.

*   *   *   *   *   *   *

SEC. 2370c–1. PROHIBITION.

(a) IN GENERAL.—Subject to subsections [(b), (c), and (d), the authorities contained in section 2321j or 2347] *(b) through (f), the authorities contained in section 2321j, 2347 and 2348* of this title or section 2763 of this title may not be used to provide assistance to, and no licenses for direct commercial sales of military equipment may be issued to, the government of a country that is clearly identified, pursuant to subsection (b), for the most recent year preceding the fiscal year in which the authorities or license would have been used or issued in the absence of a violation of sections 2370c to 2370c–2 of this title, as having governmental armed forces or government-supported armed groups, including paramilitaries, militias, or civil defense forces, that recruit and use child soldiers.

(b) IDENTIFICATION AND NOTIFICATION TO COUNTRIES IN VIOLATION OF STANDARDS.—

(1) PUBLICATION OF LIST OF FOREIGN GOVERNMENTS.—The Secretary of State shall include a list of the foreign governments that have violated the standards under sections 2370c to 2370c–2 of this title and are subject to the prohibition in subsection (a) in the report required under section 7107(b) of this title.

(2) NOTIFICATION OF FOREIGN COUNTRIES.—The Secretary of State shall formally notify any government identified pursuant to subsection (a).

(c) NATIONAL INTEREST WAIVER.—

(1) WAIVER.—The President may waive the application to a country of the prohibition in subsection (a) if the President determines that such waiver is in the national interest of the United States.

(2) PUBLICATION AND NOTIFICATION.—Not later than 45 days after each waiver is granted under paragraph (1), the President shall notify the appropriate congressional committees of the waiver and the justification for granting such waiver.

(d) REINSTATEMENT OF ASSISTANCE.—The President may provide to a country assistance otherwise prohibited under subsection (a) upon certifying to the appropriate congressional committees that the government of such country—

(1) has implemented measures that include an action plan and actual steps to come into compliance with the standards outlined in subsection (b); and

(2) has implemented policies and mechanisms to prohibit and prevent future government or government-supported use of child soldiers and to ensure that no children are recruited, conscripted, or otherwise compelled to serve as child soldiers.

(e) EXCEPTION FOR PROGRAMS DIRECTLY RELATED TO ADDRESSING THE PROBLEM OF CHILD SOLDIERS OR PROFESSIONALIZATION OF THE MILITARY.—

(1) IN GENERAL.—The President may provide assistance to a country for international military education, training, and non-lethal supplies (as defined in section 2557(d)(1)(B) of Title 10) otherwise prohibited under subsection (a) upon certifying to the appropriate congressional committees that—

(A) the government of such country is taking reasonable steps to implement effective measures to demobilize child soldiers in its forces or in government-supported paramilitaries and is taking reasonable steps within the context of its national resources to provide demobilization, rehabilitation, and reintegration assistance to those former child soldiers; and

(B) the assistance provided by the United States Government to the government of such country will go to programs that will directly support professionalization of the military.

(2) LIMITATION.—The exception under paragraph (1) may not remain in effect for a country for more than 5 years.

(f) EXCEPTION FOR PEACEKEEPING OPERATIONS.—The limitation set forth in subsection (a) that relates to section 551 of the Foreign Assistance Act of 1961 shall not apply to programs that support military professionalization, security sector reform, heightened respect for human rights, peacekeeping preparation, or the demobilization and reintegration of child soldiers.

*   *   *   *   *   *   *

CHAPTER 78—TRAFFICKING VICTIMS PROTECTION ACT

*   *   *   *   *   *   *

SEC. 7101. PURPOSES AND FINDINGS.

Historical and Statutory Notes

Pub.L. 110–457, Title II, § 225, Dec. 23, 2008, 122 Stat. 5072, provided that:

(a) RELATIONSHIP AMONG FEDERAL AND STATE LAW.—Nothing in this Act [William Wilberforce Trafficking Victims Protection Reauthorization Act of 2008, Pub.L. 110–457, Dec. 23, 2008, 122 Stat. 5044; see Tables for complete classification], the Trafficking Victims Protection Act of 2000 [Pub.L. 106–386, Div. A, §§ 101 to 113, Oct. 28, 2000, 114 Stat. 1466, which principally enacted chapter 78 of this title, 22 U.S.C.A. § 7101 et seq.; see Tables for complete classification], the Trafficking Victims Protection Reauthorization Act of 2003 [Pub.L. 108–193, Dec. 19, 2003, 117 Stat. 2875, enacting 18 U.S.C.A. § 1595, and 22 U.S.C.A. § 7109a, amending 8 U.S.C.A. §§ 1101, 1182, 1184, and 1255, 18 U.S.C.A. 1591, and 1961, 22 U.S.C.A. §§ 2152d, 7102, 7103, 7104, 7105, 7106, 7107, and 7110, enacting provisions set out as notes under this section and 22 U.S.C.A. § 7103, and repealing provisions set out as notes under 22 U.S.C.A. § 7103], the Trafficking Victims Protection Reauthorization Act of 2005 [Pub.L. 109–164, Jan. 10, 2006, 119 Stat. 3558, enacting 18 U.S.C.A. § 2428, chapter 212A of Title 18, 18 U.S.C.A. § 3271 et seq., 22 U.S.C.A. §§ 7111 and 7112, and part O of subchapter III of chapter 136 of Title 42, 42 U.S.C.A. § 14044 et seq., amending 18 U.S.C.A. §§ 1956 and 1961, and 22 U.S.C.A. §§ 4028, 7103, 7104, 7105, 7106, 7107, 7109a, and 7110, and enacting provisions set out as notes under this section and 22 U.S.C.A. §§ 7105 and 7106], chapters 77 and 117 of title 18, United States Code [18 U.S.C.A. § 1581 et seq. and 18 U.S.C.A. § 2421 et seq.], or any model law issued by the Department of Justice to carry out the purposes of any of the aforementioned statutes—

(1) may be construed to treat prostitution as a valid form of employment under Federal law; or

(2) shall preempt, supplant, or limit the effect of any State or Federal criminal law.

(b) MODEL STATE CRIMINAL PROVISIONS.—In addition to any model State antitrafficking statutes in effect on the date of the enactment of this Act [Dec. 23, 2008], the Attorney General shall facilitate the promulgation of a model State statute that—

(1) furthers a comprehensive approach to investigation and prosecution through modernization of State and local prostitution and pandering statutes; [and]

(2) protects children exploited through prostitution by including safe harbor provisions that—

(A) treat an individual under 18 years of age who has been arrested for engaging in, or attempting to engage in, a sexual act with another person in exchange for monetary compensation as a victim of a severe form of trafficking in persons;

(B) prohibit the charging or prosecution of an individual described in subparagraph (A) for a prostitution offense;

(C) require the referral of an individual described in subparagraph (A) to appropriate service providers, including comprehensive service or community-based programs that provide assistance to child victims of commercial sexual exploitation; and

(D) provide that an individual described in subparagraph (A) shall not be required to prove fraud, force, or coercion in order to receive the protections described under this paragraph;

[(2)] (3) is based in part on the provisions of the Act of August 15, 1935 (49 Stat. 651; D.C. Code 22–2701 et seq.) [Act Aug. 15, 1935, c. 546, 49 Stat. 651] (relating to prostitution and pandering).

(c) DISTRIBUTION.—The model statute described in subsection (b) and the text of chapter 27 of the Criminal Code of the District of Columbia (D.C. Code 22–2701 et seq.) shall be—

(1) posted on the website of the Department of Justice; and

(2) distributed to the Attorney General of each State.

*   *   *   *   *   *   *

SEC. 7102. DEFINITIONS.

In this chapter:

(1) ABUSE OR THREATENED ABUSE OF LAW OR LEGAL PROCESS.—The term "abuse or threatened abuse of the legal process" means the use or threatened use of a law or legal process, whether administrative, civil, or criminal, in any manner or for any purpose for which the law was not designed, in order to exert pressure on another person to cause that person to take some action or refrain from taking some action.

[(1)] *(2)* APPROPRIATE CONGRESSIONAL COMMITTEES.—The term "appropriate congressional committees" means the Committee on Foreign Relations and the Committee on the Judiciary of the Senate and the Committee on Foreign Affairs and the Committee on the Judiciary of the House of Representatives.

[(2)] *(3)* COERCION.—The term "coercion" means—

(A) threats of serious harm to or physical restraint against any person;

(B) any scheme, plan, or pattern intended to cause a person to believe that failure to perform an act would result in serious harm to or physical restraint against any person; or

(C) the abuse or threatened abuse of the legal process.

[(3)] *(4)* COMMERCIAL SEX ACT.—The term "commercial sex act" means any sex act on account of which anything of value is given to or received by any person.

[(4)] *(5)* DEBT BONDAGE.—The term "debt bondage" means the status or condition of a debtor arising from a pledge by the debtor of his or her personal services or of those of a person under his or her control as a security for debt, if the value of those services as reasonably assessed is not applied toward the liquidation of the debt or the length and nature of those services are not respectively limited and defined.

[(5)] *(6)* INVOLUNTARY SERVITUDE.—The term "involuntary servitude" includes a condition of servitude induced by means of—

(A) any scheme, plan, or pattern intended to cause a person to believe that, if the person did not enter into or continue in such condition, that person or another person would suffer serious harm or physical restraint; or

(B) the abuse or threatened abuse of the legal process.

[(6)] *(7)* MINIMUM STANDARDS FOR THE ELIMINATION OF TRAFFICKING.—The term "minimum standards for the elimination of trafficking" means the standards set forth in section 7106 of this title.

[(7)] *(8)* NONHUMANITARIAN, NONTRADE-RELATED FOREIGN ASSISTANCE.—The term "nonhumanitarian, nontrade-related foreign assistance" means—

(A) any assistance under the Foreign Assistance Act of 1961 [22 U.S.C.A. § 2151 et seq.], other than—

(i) assistance under chapter 4 of part II of that Act [22 U.S.C.A. § 2346 et seq.] in support of programs of nongovernmental organizations that is made available for any program, project, or activity eligible for assistance under chapter 1 of part I of that Act [22 U.S.C.A. § 2151 et seq.];

(ii) assistance under chapter 8 of part I of that Act [22 U.S.C.A. § 2291 et seq.];

(iii) any other narcotics-related assistance under part I of that Act [22 U.S.C.A. § 2151 et seq.] or under chapter 4 or 5 part II of that Act [22 U.S.C.A. § 2346 et seq., 2347 et seq.], but any such assistance provided under this clause shall be subject to the prior notification procedures applicable to reprogrammings pursuant to section 634A of that Act [22 U.S.C.A. § 2394–1];

(iv) disaster relief assistance, including any assistance under chapter 9 of part I of that Act [22 U.S.C.A. § 2292 et seq.];

(v) antiterrorism assistance under chapter 8 of part II of that Act [22 U.S.C.A. § 1349aa et seq.];

(vi) assistance for refugees;

(vii) humanitarian and other development assistance in support of programs of nongovernmental organizations under chapters 1 and 10 of that Act;

(viii) programs under title IV of chapter 2 of part I of that Act [22 U.S.C.A. § 2191 et seq.], relating to the Overseas Private Investment Corporation; and

(ix) other programs involving trade-related or humanitarian assistance; and

(B) sales, or financing on any terms, under the Arms Export Control Act [22 U.S.C.A. § 2751 et seq.], other than sales or financing provided for narcotics-related purposes following notification in accordance with the prior notification procedures applicable to reprogrammings pursuant to section 634A of the Foreign Assistance Act of 1961 [22 U.S.C.A. § 2394–1].

[(8)] *(9)* SEVERE FORMS OF TRAFFICKING IN PERSONS.—The term "severe forms of trafficking in persons" means—

(A) sex trafficking in which a commercial sex act is induced by force, fraud, or coercion, or in which the person induced to perform such act has not attained 18 years of age; or

(B) the recruitment, harboring, transportation, provision, or obtaining of a person for labor or services, through the use of force, fraud, or coercion for the purpose of subjection to involuntary servitude, peonage, debt bondage, or slavery.

[(9)] *(10)* SEX TRAFFICKING.—The term "sex trafficking" means the recruitment, harboring, transportation, provision, or obtaining of a person for the purpose of a commercial sex act.

[(10)] *(11)* STATE.—The term "State" means each of the several States of the United States, the District of Columbia, the Commonwealth of Puerto Rico, the United States Virgin Islands, Guam, American Samoa, the Commonwealth of the Northern Mariana Islands, and territories and possessions of the United States.

[(11)] *(12)* TASK FORCE.—The term "Task Force" means the Interagency Task Force to Monitor and Combat Trafficking established under section 7103 of this title.

[(12)] *(13)* UNITED STATES.—The term "United States" means the fifty States of the United States, the District of Columbia, the Commonwealth of Puerto Rico, the Virgin Islands, American Samoa, Guam, the Commonwealth of the Northern Mariana Islands, and the territories and possessions of the United States.

[(13)] *(14)* VICTIM OF A SEVERE FORM OF TRAFFICKING.—The term "victim of a severe form of trafficking" means a person subject to an act or practice described in [paragraph (8)] *paragraph (9)*.

[(14)] *(15)* VICTIM OF TRAFFICKING.—The term "victim of trafficking" means a person subjected to an act or practice described in [paragraph (8) or (9)] *paragraph (9) or (10)*.

*   *   *   *   *   *   *

SEC. 7103. INTERAGENCY TASK FORCE TO MONITOR AND COMBAT TRAFFICKING.

(a) ESTABLISHMENT.—The President shall establish an Interagency Task Force to Monitor and Combat Trafficking.

(b) APPOINTMENT.—The President shall appoint the members of the Task Force, which shall include the Secretary of State, the Administrator of the United States Agency for International Development, the Attorney General, the Secretary of Labor, the Secretary of Health and Human Services, the Director of National Intelligence, the Secretary of Defense, the Secretary of Homeland Security, the Secretary of Education, and such other officials as may be designated by the President.

(c) CHAIRMAN.—The Task Force shall be chaired by the Secretary of State.

(d) ACTIVITIES OF THE TASK FORCE.—The Task Force shall carry out the following activities:

(1) Coordinate the implementation of this chapter.

(2) Measure and evaluate progress of the United States and other countries in the areas of trafficking prevention, protection, and assistance to victims of trafficking, and prosecution and enforcement against traffickers, including the role of public corruption in facilitating trafficking. The Task Force shall have primary responsibility for assisting the Secretary of State in the preparation of the reports described in section 7107 of this title.

(3) Expand interagency procedures to collect and organize data, including significant research and resource information

on domestic and international trafficking. Any data collection procedures established under this subsection shall respect the confidentiality of victims of trafficking.

(4) Engage in efforts to facilitate cooperation among countries of origin, transit, and destination. Such efforts shall aim to strengthen local and regional capacities to prevent trafficking, prosecute traffickers and assist trafficking victims, and shall include initiatives to enhance cooperative efforts between destination countries and countries of origin and assist in the appropriate reintegration of stateless victims of trafficking.

(5) Examine the role of the international "sex tourism" industry in the trafficking of persons and in the sexual exploitation of women and children around the world.

(6) Engage in consultation and advocacy with governmental and nongovernmental organizations, among other entities, to advance the purposes of this chapter, *and make reasonable efforts to distribute information to enable all relevant Federal Government agencies to publicize the National Human Trafficking Resource Center Hotline on their websites, in all headquarters offices, and in all field offices throughout the United States.*

(7) Not later than May 1, 2004, and annually thereafter, the Attorney General shall submit to the Committee on Ways and Means, the Committee on Foreign Affairs, and the Committee on the Judiciary of the House of Representatives and the Committee on Finance, the Committee on Foreign Relations, and the Committee on the Judiciary of the Senate, a report on Federal agencies that are implementing any provision of this chapter, or any amendment made by this chapter, which shall include, at a minimum, information on—

(A) the number of persons who received benefits or other services under subsections (b) and (f) of section 7105 of this title in connection with programs or activities funded or administered by the Secretary of Health and Human Services, the Secretary of Labor, the Attorney General, the Board of Directors of the Legal Services Corporation, and other appropriate Federal agencies during the preceding fiscal year;

⟦(B) the number of persons who have been granted continued presence in the United States under section 7105(c)(3) of this title during the preceding fiscal year;

⟦(C) the number of persons who have applied for, been granted, or been denied a visa or otherwise provided status under section 1101(a)(15)(T)(i) of Title 8 during the preceding fiscal year;⟧

(B) the number of persons who have been granted continued presence in the United States under section 107(c)(3) during the preceding fiscal year and the mean and median time taken to adjudicate applications submitted under such section, including the time from the receipt of an application by law enforcement to the issuance of continued presence, and a description of any efforts being taken to reduce the adjudication and processing time while ensuring the safe and competent processing of the applications;

(C) the number of persons who have applied for, been granted, or been denied a visa or otherwise provided status under subparagraph (T)(i) or (U)(i) of section 101(a)(15) of the Immigration and Nationality Act (8 U.S.C. 1101(a)(15)) during the preceding fiscal year;

(D) the number of persons who have applied for, been granted, or been denied a visa or status under clause (ii) of section 101(a)(15)(T) of the Immigration and Nationality Act (8 U.S.C. 1101(a)(15)(T)) during the preceding fiscal year, broken down by the number of such persons described in subclauses (I), (II), and (III) of such clause (ii);

(E) the amount of Federal funds expended in direct benefits paid to individuals described in subparagraph (D) in conjunction with T visa status;

(F) the number of persons who have applied for, been granted, or been denied a visa or status under section 101(a)(15)(U)(i) of the Immigration and Nationality Act (8 U.S.C. 1101(a)(15)(U)(i)) during the preceding fiscal year;

(G) the mean and median time in which it takes to adjudicate applications submitted under the provisions of law set forth in subparagraph (C), including the time between the receipt of an application and the issuance of a visa and work authorization;

(H) any efforts being taken to reduce the adjudication and processing time, while ensuring the safe and competent processing of the applications;

[(D)] *(I)* the number of persons who have been charged or convicted under one or more of sections 1581, 1583, 1584, 1589, 1590, 1591, 1592, or 1594 of Title 18, during the preceding fiscal year and the sentences imposed against each such person;

[(E)] *(J)* the amount, recipient, and purpose of each grant issued by any Federal agency to carry out the purposes of sections 7104 and 7105 of this title, or section 2152d of this title, during the preceding fiscal year;

[(F)] *(K)* the nature of training conducted pursuant to section 7105(c)(4) of this title during the preceding fiscal year;

[(G)] *(L)* the amount, recipient, and purpose of each grant under sections 14044a and 14044c of Title 42;

[(H)]] *(M)* activities by the Department of Defense to combat trafficking in persons, including—

(i) educational efforts for, and disciplinary actions taken against, members of the United States Armed Forces;

(ii) the development of materials used to train the armed forces of foreign countries[; and]*;*

(iii) all known trafficking in persons cases reported to the Under Secretary of Defense for Personnel and Readiness;

[(iii)] *(iv)* efforts to ensure that United States Government contractors and their employees or United States Government subcontractors and their employees do not engage in trafficking in persons[;]*; and*

(v) all trafficking in persons activities of contractors reported to the Under Secretary of Defense for Acquisition Technology and Logistics;

[(I)] *(N)* activities or actions by Federal departments and agencies to enforce—

(i) section 7104(g) of this title and any similar law, regulation, or policy relating to United States Government contractors and their employees or United States Government subcontractors and their employees that engage in severe forms of trafficking in persons, the procurement of commercial sex acts, or the use of forced labor, including debt bondage;

(ii) section 1307 of Title 19; relating to prohibition on importation of convict-made goods), including any determinations by the Secretary of Homeland Security to waive the restrictions of such section; and

(iii) prohibitions on the procurement by the United States Government of items or services produced by slave labor, consistent with Executive Order 13107 (December 10, 1998); [and]

[(J)] *(O)* the activities undertaken by the Senior Policy Operating Group to carry out its responsibilities under [subsection (f)] *subsection g* of this section[.]*;*

(P) the activities undertaken by Federal agencies to train appropriate State, tribal, and local government and law enforcement officials to identify victims of severe forms of trafficking, including both sex and labor trafficking;

(Q) the activities undertaken by Federal agencies in cooperation with State, tribal, and local law enforcement officials to identify, investigate, and prosecute offenses under sections 1581, 1583, 1584, 1589, 1590, 1592, and 1594 of title 18, United States Code, or equivalent State offenses, including, in each fiscal year—

(i) the number, age, gender, country of origin, and citizenship status of victims identified for each offense;

(ii) the number of individuals charged, and the number of individuals convicted, under each offense;

(iii) the number of individuals referred for prosecution for State offenses, including offenses relating to the purchasing of commercial sex acts;

(iv) the number of victims granted continued presence in the United States under section 107(c)(3); and

(v) the number of victims granted a visa or otherwise provided status under subparagraph (T)(i) or (U)(i) of section 101(a)(15) of the Immigration and Nationality Act (8 U.S.C. 1101(a)(15)); and

(R) the activities undertaken by the Department of Justice and the Department of Health and Human Services to meet the specific needs of minor victims of domestic trafficking, including actions taken pursuant to subsection (f) and section 202(a) of the Trafficking Victims Protection Reauthorization Act of 2005 (42 U.S.C. 14044(a)), and the steps taken to increase cooperation among Federal agencies

to ensure the effective and efficient use of programs for which the victims are eligible.

(e) OFFICE TO MONITOR AND COMBAT TRAFFICKING.—

(1) IN GENERAL.—The Secretary of State shall establish within the Department of State an Office to Monitor and Combat Trafficking, which shall provide assistance to the Task Force. Any such Office shall be headed by a Director, who shall be appointed by the President, by and with the advice and consent of the Senate, with the rank of Ambassador-at-Large. The Director shall have the primary responsibility for assisting the Secretary of State in carrying out the purposes of this chapter and may have additional responsibilities as determined by the Secretary. The Director shall consult with nongovernmental organizations and multilateral organizations, and with trafficking victims or other affected persons. The Director shall have the authority to take evidence in public hearings or by other means. The agencies represented on the Task Force are authorized to provide staff to the Office on a nonreimbursable basis.

⟦(2) COORDINATION OF CERTAIN ACTIVITIES.—

⟦(A) PARTNERSHIPS.—The Director, in coordination and cooperation with other officials at the Department of State involved in corporate responsibility, the Deputy Under Secretary for International Affairs of the Department of Labor, and other relevant officials of the United States Government, shall promote, build, and sustain partnerships between the United States Government and private entities (including foundations, universities, corporations, community-based organizations, and other nongovernmental organizations) to ensure that—

⟦(i) United States citizens do not use any item, product, or material produced or extracted with the use of labor from victims of severe forms of trafficking; and

⟦(ii) such entities do not contribute to trafficking in persons involving sexual exploitation.⟧

⟦(B)⟧ *(2)* UNITED STATES ASSISTANCE.—The Director shall be responsible for—

⟦(i)⟧ *(A)* all policy, funding, and programming decisions regarding funds made available for trafficking in persons programs that are centrally controlled by the Office to Monitor and Combat Trafficking; and

⟦(ii)⟧ *(B)* coordinating any trafficking in persons programs of the Department of State or the United States Agency for International Development that are not centrally controlled by the Director.

(f) REGIONAL STRATEGIES FOR COMBATING TRAFFICKING IN PERSONS.—Each regional bureau in the Department of State shall contribute to the realization of the anti-trafficking goals and objectives of the Secretary of State. By June 30 of each year, in cooperation with the Office to Monitor and Combat Trafficking, each regional bureau shall submit a list of anti-trafficking goals and objectives for each country in its geographic area of responsibility. Host governments shall be informed of the goals and objectives for their particular country by June 30 and, to the extent possible, host govern-

ment officials should contribute to the drafting of the goals and objectives.

[(f)] *(g)* SENIOR POLICY OPERATING GROUP.—

(1) ESTABLISHMENT.—There shall be established within the executive branch a Senior Policy Operating Group.

(2) MEMBERSHIP; RELATED MATTERS.—

(A) IN GENERAL.—The Operating Group shall consist of the senior officials designated as representatives of the appointed members of the Task Force (pursuant to Executive Order No. 13257 of February 13, 2002).

(B) CHAIRPERSON.—The Operating Group shall be chaired by the Director of the Office to Monitor and Combat Trafficking of the Department of State.

(C) MEETINGS.—The Operating Group shall meet on a regular basis at the call of the Chairperson.

(3) DUTIES.—The Operating Group shall coordinate activities of Federal departments and agencies regarding policies (including grants and grant policies) involving the international trafficking in persons and the implementation of this chapter.

(4) AVAILABILITY OF INFORMATION.—Each Federal department or agency represented on the Operating Group shall fully share all information with such Group regarding the department or agency's plans, before and after final agency decisions are made, on all matters relating to grants, grant policies, and other significant actions regarding the international trafficking in persons and the implementation of this division.

(5) REGULATIONS.—Not later than 90 days after December 19, 2003, the President shall promulgate regulations to implement this section, including regulations to carry out paragraph (4).

SEC. 7103A. CREATING, BUILDING, AND STRENGTHENING PARTNERSHIPS AGAINST SIGNIFICANT TRAFFICKING IN PERSONS.

(a) DECLARATION OF PURPOSE.—The purpose of this section is to promote collaboration and cooperation—

(1) between the United States Government and governments listed on the annual Trafficking in Persons Report;

(2) between foreign governments and civil society actors; and

(3) between the United States Government and private sector entities.

(b) PARTNERSHIPS.—The Director, in coordination and cooperation with other officials at the Department of State involved in corporate responsibility and global partnerships, the Deputy Under Secretary for International Affairs of the Department of Labor, and other relevant officials of the United States Government, shall promote, build, and sustain partnerships between the United States Government and private entities, including foundations, universities, corporations, community-based organizations, and other nongovernmental organizations, to ensure that—

(1) United States citizens do not use any item, product, or material produced or extracted with the use and labor from victims of severe forms of trafficking; and

(2) such entities do not contribute to trafficking in persons involving sexual exploitation.

(c) ADDITIONAL MEASURES TO ENHANCE ANTI-TRAFFICKING RE-SPONSE AND CAPACITY.—*The President shall establish and carry out programs with foreign governments and civil society to enhance anti-trafficking response and capacity, including—*

(1) technical assistance and other support to improve the capacity of foreign governments to investigate, identify, and carry out inspections of private entities, including labor recruitment centers, at which trafficking victims may be exploited, particularly exploitation involving forced and child labor;

(2) technical assistance and other support for foreign governments and nongovernmental organizations to provide immigrant populations with information, in the native languages of the major immigrant groups of such populations, regarding the rights of such populations in the foreign country and local in-country nongovernmental organization-operated hotlines;

(3) technical assistance to provide legal frameworks and other programs to foreign governments and nongovernmental organizations to ensure that—

(A) foreign migrant workers are provided the same protection as nationals of the foreign country;

(B) labor recruitment firms are regulated; and

(C) workers providing domestic services in households are provided protection under labor rights laws; and

(4) assistance to foreign governments to register vulnerable populations as citizens or nationals of the country to reduce the ability of traffickers to exploit such populations, where possible under domestic law.

(d) PROGRAM TO ADDRESS EMERGENCY SITUATIONS.—*The Secretary of State, acting through the Director of the Office to Monitor and Combat Trafficking in Persons, is authorized to establish a fund to assist foreign governments in meeting unexpected, urgent needs in prevention of trafficking in persons, protection of victims, and prosecution of trafficking offenders.*

(e) CHILD PROTECTION COMPACTS.—

(1) IN GENERAL.—*The Secretary of State, acting through the Director of the Office to Monitor and Combat Trafficking in Persons and in consultation with the Bureau of Democracy, Human Rights, and Labor, the Bureau of International Labor Affairs of the Department of Labor, the United States Agency for International Development, and other relevant agencies, is authorized to provide assistance under this section for each country that enters into a child protection compact with the United States to support policies and programs that—*

(A) prevent and respond to violence, exploitation, and abuse against children; and

(B) measurably reduce severe forms of trafficking in children by building sustainable and effective systems of justice and protection.

(2) ELEMENTS.—*A child protection compact under this subsection shall establish a multi- year plan for achieving shared objectives in furtherance of the purposes of this Act, and shall describe—*

(A) the specific objectives the foreign government and the United States Government expect to achieve during the term of the compact;

(B) the responsibilities of the foreign government and the United States Government in the achievement of such objectives;

(C) the particular programs or initiatives to be undertaken in the achievement of such objectives and the amount of funding to be allocated to each program or initiative by both countries;

(D) regular outcome indicators to monitor and measure progress toward achieving such objectives; and

(E) a multi-year financial plan, including the estimated amount of contributions by the United States Government and the foreign government, and proposed mechanisms to implement the plan and provide oversight.

(3) FORM OF ASSISTANCE.—Assistance under this subsection may be provided in the form of grants, cooperative agreements, or contracts to or with national governments, regional or local governmental units, or non-governmental organizations or private entities with expertise in the protection of victims of severe forms of trafficking in persons.

(4) ELIGIBLE COUNTRIES.—The Secretary of State, acting through the Office to Monitor and Combat Trafficking in Persons, and in consultation with the agencies set forth in paragraph (1) and relevant officers of the Department of Justice, shall select countries with which to enter into child protection compacts. The selection of countries under this paragraph shall be based on—

(A) the selection criteria set forth in paragraph (5); and

(B) objective, documented, and quantifiable indicators, to the maximum extent possible.

(5) SELECTION CRITERIA.—A country shall be selected under paragraph (4) on the basis of—

(A) a documented high prevalence of trafficking in persons within the country; and

(B) demonstrated political will and sustained commitment by the government of such country to undertake meaningful measures to address severe forms of trafficking in persons, including protection of victims and the enactment and enforcement of anti-trafficking laws against perpetrators.

(6) SUSPENSION AND TERMINATION OF ASSISTANCE.—

(A) IN GENERAL.—The Secretary may suspend or terminate assistance provided under this subsection in whole or in part for a country or entity if the Secretary determines that—

(i) the country or entity is engaged in activities that are contrary to the national security interests of the United States;

(ii) the country or entity has engaged in a pattern of actions inconsistent with the criteria used to determine the eligibility of the country or entity, as the case may be; or

(iii) the country or entity has failed to adhere to its responsibilities under the Compact.

(B) REINSTATEMENT.—The Secretary may reinstate assistance for a country or entity suspended or terminated under this paragraph only if the Secretary determines that the country or entity has demonstrated a commitment to correcting each condition for which assistance was suspended or terminated under subparagraph (A).

SEC. 7104. PREVENTION OF TRAFFICKING.

(a) ECONOMIC ALTERNATIVES TO PREVENT AND DETER TRAFFICKING.—The President shall establish and carry out international initiatives to enhance economic opportunity for potential victims of trafficking as a method to deter trafficking. Such initiatives may include—

(1) microcredit lending programs, training in business development, skills training, and job counseling;

(2) programs to promote women's participation in economic decisionmaking;

(3) programs to keep children, especially girls, in elementary and secondary schools, and to educate persons who have been victims of trafficking;

(4) development of educational curricula regarding the dangers of trafficking; and

(5) grants to nongovernmental organizations to accelerate and advance the political, economic, social, and educational roles and capacities of women in their countries.

(b) PUBLIC AWARENESS AND INFORMATION.—The President, acting through the Secretary of Labor, the Secretary of Health and Human Services, the Attorney General, and the Secretary of State, shall establish and carry out programs to increase public awareness, particularly among potential victims of trafficking, of the dangers of trafficking and the protections that are available for victims of trafficking.

(c) BORDER INTERDICTION.—The President shall establish and carry out programs of border interdiction outside the United States. Such programs shall include providing grants to foreign nongovernmental organizations that provide for transit shelters operating at key border crossings and that help train survivors of trafficking in persons to educate and train border guards and officials, and other local law enforcement officials, to identify traffickers and victims of severe forms of trafficking, and the appropriate manner in which to treat such victims. Such programs shall also include, to the extent appropriate, monitoring by such survivors of trafficking in persons of the implementation of border interdiction programs, including helping in the identification of such victims to stop the cross-border transit of victims. The President shall ensure that any program established under this subsection provides the opportunity for any trafficking victim who is freed to return to his or her previous residence if the victim so chooses.

(d) INTERNATIONAL MEDIA.—The President shall establish and carry out programs that support the production of television and radio programs, including documentaries, to inform vulnerable populations overseas of the dangers of trafficking, and to increase awareness of the public in countries of destination regarding the slave-like practices and other human rights abuses involved in trafficking, including fostering linkages between individuals working in the media in different countries to determine the best methods for informing such populations through such media.

(e) REGIONAL ANTI-TRAFFICKING IN PERSONS OFFICERS.—Under the authority, direction, and control of the President, the Secretary of State, in accordance with the provisions of this Act, and in order to promote effective bilateral and regional anti-trafficking diplomacy, public diplomacy initiatives, and coordination of programs, is authorized—

(1) to appoint, at United States embassies, anti-trafficking in persons officers, who shall collaborate with other countries to eliminate human trafficking; and

(2) to assign the officers appointed under paragraph (1) to fulfill tasks such as—

(A) expanding the anti-trafficking efforts of the Office to Monitor and Combat Trafficking in Persons of the Department of State, including—

(i) maintaining direct contact with the Office to Monitor and Combat Trafficking in Persons; and

(ii) undertaking tasks recommended by the Director of the Office to Monitor and Combat Trafficking in Persons;

(B) monitoring trafficking trends in the region;

(C) assessing compliance with the provisions of this Act;

(D) determining and furthering effective anti-trafficking programs and partnerships with foreign governments and foreign nongovernmental organizations;

(E) strengthening diplomatic outreach on trafficking in persons; and

(F) assisting and advising United States embassies overseas on their input to the Office to Monitor and Combat Trafficking in Persons for the preparation of the annual Trafficking in Persons Report.

[(e)] *(f)* COMBATING INTERNATIONAL SEX TOURISM.—

(1) DEVELOPMENT AND DISSEMINATION OF MATERIALS.—The President, pursuant to such regulations as may be prescribed, shall ensure that materials are developed and disseminated to alert travelers that sex tourism (as described in subsections (b) through (f) of section 2423 of Title 18) is illegal, will be prosecuted, and presents dangers to those involved. Such materials shall be disseminated to individuals traveling to foreign destinations where the President determines that sex tourism is significant.

(2) MONITORING OF COMPLIANCE.—The President shall monitor compliance with the requirements of paragraph (1).

(3) FEASIBILITY REPORT.—Not later than 180 days after December 19, 2003, the President shall transmit to the Committee on International Relations of the House of Representatives and the Committee on Foreign Affairs of the Senate a report that describes the feasibility of such United States Government materials being disseminated through public-private partnerships to individuals traveling to foreign destinations.

[(f)] *(g)* CONSULTATION REQUIREMENT.—The President shall consult with appropriate nongovernmental organizations with respect to the establishment and conduct of initiatives and programs described in subsections (a) through (e) of this section.

[(g)] *(h)* TERMINATION OF CERTAIN GRANTS, CONTRACTS AND CO-OPERATIVE AGREEMENTS.—

[The President] *(1) IN GENERAL.—The President* shall ensure that any grant, contract, or cooperative agreement provided or entered into by a Federal department or agency under which funds are to be provided to a private entity, in whole or in part, shall include a condition that authorizes the department or agency to terminate the grant, contract, or cooperative agreement, without penalty, if the grantee or any subgrantee, or the contractor or any [subcontractor (i) engages in severe forms of trafficking in persons or has procured a commercial sex act during the period of time that the grant, contract, or cooperative agreement is in effect, or (ii) uses forced labor in the performance of the grant, contract, or cooperative agreement.] *subcontractor engages in, or uses labor recruiters or brokers who engage in, acts related to trafficking in persons, the procurement of commercial sex acts, or the use of forced labor in the performance of the grant, contract, or cooperative agreement, including, if in furtherance of such acts—*

(A) destroying, concealing, removing, or confiscating an employee's immigration documents without the employee's consent;

(B) failing to assist with the repatriation of an employee upon the end of employment, unless the employee is a victim of human trafficking seeking victim services or legal redress in the country of employment;

(C) placing an employee in a location or occupation other than the location or occupation that was indicated to the employee when the employee was recruited, without the concurrence of the employee;

(D) charging recruited employees placement fees equal to or greater than the employee's annual salary or half the employee's total anticipated pay, whichever is less; and

(E) any other activities that support or promote trafficking in persons, the procurement of commercial sex acts, or the use of forced labor in the performance of the grant, contract, or cooperative agreement.

(2) CONTRACT COMPLIANCE PLAN.—

(A) COMPLIANCE PLAN AND CERTIFICATION OF SUB-CONTRACT REVIEW.—The head of a Federal department or agency may not make or enter into a grant, contract, or cooperative agreement valued at $1,000,000 or more if performance will predominantly be conducted overseas in support of contingency operations, unless a duly designated representative of the entity receiving such grant, contract, or cooperative agreement certifies to the contracting officer, after having conducted due diligence, that—

(i) the contracting entity has implemented a plan to prevent the activities described in subparagraphs (A)

through (E) of paragraph (1) and is in compliance with such plan; and

(ii) to the best of such representative's knowledge, neither the contracting entity nor any subgrantee or subcontractor holding a subgrant or subcontract under such grant, contract, or cooperative agreement valued at $1,000,000 or more, is engaged in any of the activities described in such subparagraphs.

(B) CONTRACT EVALUATION.—

(i) IN GENERAL.—If the contracting officer for a grant, contract, or cooperative agreement described under subparagraph (A) receives any report that a contracting entity, or any subcontractor or subgrantee, has engaged in an activity described in paragraph (1), including reports from a contracting officer representative, an inspector general, an auditor, or any other official source, the contracting officer may, before renewing any remaining options for such grant, contract, or cooperative agreement, or the grant, contract, or cooperative agreement itself, attempt to resolve the areas of noncompliance or unsatisfactory performance and modify such grant, contract, or cooperative agreement to prevent future occurrences of such noncompliance or unsatisfactory performance.

(ii) EFFECT OF CONTINUED NONCOMPLIANCE.—If the contracting officer determines that the noncompliance or unsatisfactory performance under the grant, contract, or cooperative agreement described in clause (i) cannot be resolved and prevented in the future, the contracting officer—

(I) may not renew any remaining options for such grant, contract, or cooperative agreement, or the grant, contract, or cooperative agreement itself, with such contracting entity; and

(II) may terminate the grant, contract, or cooperative agreement without penalty if such grant, contract, or cooperative agreement was made or entered into after the effective date of this paragraph.

(iii) INCLUSION OF CREDIBLE REPORTS.—A contracting officer may enter in the past performance evaluation of a contractor any reports, determined to be credible by the contracting officer, that any entity has engaged in any activity described in subparagraphs (A) through (E) of paragraph (1), including reports from a contracting officer representative, an inspector general, an auditor, or any other official source.

(3) RULE OF CONSTRUCTION.—Nothing in this subsection may be construed as superseding, restricting, or limiting the application of any Federal contracting law or regulation.

[(h)] *(i)* PREVENTION OF TRAFFICKING IN CONJUNCTION WITH POST-CONFLICT AND HUMANITARIAN EMERGENCY ASSISTANCE.—The United States Agency for International Development, the Department of State, and the Department of Defense shall incorporate anti-trafficking and protection measures for vulnerable populations, particularly women and children, into their post-conflict and humanitarian emergency assistance and program activities.

[(i)] *(j)* ADDITIONAL MEASURES TO PREVENT AND DETER TRAFFICKING.—The President shall establish and carry out programs to prevent and deter trafficking in persons, including—

(1) technical assistance and other support to improve the capacity of foreign governments to investigate, identify, and carry out inspections of private entities, including labor recruitment centers, at which trafficking victims may be exploited, particularly exploitation involving forced and child labor;

(2) technical assistance and other support for foreign governments and nongovernmental organizations to provide immigrant populations with information, in the native languages of the major immigrant groups of such populations, regarding the rights of such populations in the foreign country and local in-country nongovernmental organization-operated hotlines;

(3) technical assistance to provide legal frameworks and other programs to foreign governments and nongovernmental organizations to ensure that—

(A) foreign migrant workers are provided the same protection as nationals of the foreign country;

(B) labor recruitment firms are regulated; and

(C) workers providing domestic services in households are provided protection under labor rights laws; and

(4) assistance to foreign governments to register vulnerable populations as citizens or nationals of the country to reduce the ability of traffickers to exploit such populations.

(k) PREVENTION OF CHILD TRAFFICKING THROUGH CHILD MARRIAGE.—The Secretary of State shall establish and implement a multi-year, multi-sectoral strategy—

(1) to prevent child marriage;

(2) to promote the empowerment of girls at risk of child marriage in developing countries;

(3) that should address the unique needs, vulnerabilities, and potential of girls younger than 18 years of age in developing countries;

(4) that targets areas in developing countries with high prevalence of child marriage; and

(5) that includes diplomatic and programmatic initiatives.

SEC. 7105. PROTECTION AND ASSISTANCE FOR VICTIMS OF TRAFFICKING.

(a) ASSISTANCE FOR VICTIMS IN OTHER COUNTRIES.—

(1) IN GENERAL.—The Secretary of State and the Administrator of the United States Agency for International Development, in consultation with appropriate nongovernmental organizations, shall establish and carry out programs and initiatives in foreign countries to assist in the safe integration, reintegration, or resettlement, as appropriate, of victims of trafficking. Such programs and initiatives shall be designed to meet the appropriate assistance needs of such persons and their children, as identified by the Task Force, and shall be carried out in a manner which takes into account the cross-border, regional, and transnational aspects of trafficking in per-

sons. In addition, such programs and initiatives shall, to the maximum extent practicable, include the following:

(A) Support for local in-country nongovernmental organization-operated hotlines, culturally and linguistically appropriate protective shelters, and regional and international nongovernmental organization networks and databases on trafficking, including support to assist nongovernmental organizations in establishing service centers and systems that are mobile and extend beyond large cities.

(B) Support for nongovernmental organizations and advocates to provide legal, social, and other services and assistance to trafficked individuals, particularly those individuals in detention, and by facilitating contact between relevant foreign government agencies and such nongovernmental organizations to facilitate cooperation between the foreign governments and such organizations.

(C) Education and training for trafficked women and girls.

(D) The safe integration or reintegration of trafficked individuals into an appropriate community or family, with full respect for the wishes, dignity, and safety of the trafficked individual.

(E) Support for developing or increasing programs to assist families of victims in locating, repatriating, and treating their trafficked family members, in assisting the voluntary repatriation of these family members or their integration or resettlement into appropriate communities, and in providing them with treatment.

(F) In cooperation and coordination with relevant organizations, such as the United Nations High Commissioner for Refugees, the International Organization for Migration, and private nongovernmental organizations that contract with, or receive grants from, the United States Government to assist refugees and internally displaced persons, support for—

(i) increased protections for refugees and internally displaced persons, including outreach and education efforts to prevent such refugees and internally displaced persons from being exploited by traffickers; and

(ii) performance of best interest determinations for unaccompanied and separated children who come to the attention of the United Nations High Commissioner for Refugees, its partner organizations, or any organization that contracts with the Department of State in order to identify child trafficking victims and to assist their safe integration, reintegration, and resettlement.

(2) ADDITIONAL REQUIREMENT.—In establishing and conducting programs and initiatives described in paragraph (1), the Secretary of State and the Administrator of the United States Agency for International Development shall take all appropriate steps to enhance cooperative efforts among foreign countries, including countries of origin of victims of trafficking,

to assist in the integration, reintegration, or resettlement, as appropriate, of victims of trafficking, including stateless victims. In carrying out this paragraph, the Secretary and the Administrator shall take all appropriate steps to ensure that cooperative efforts among foreign countries are undertaken on a regional basis *and shall brief Congress annually on such efforts.*

* * * * * * *

(c) TRAFFICKING VICTIM REGULATIONS.—Not later than 180 days after October 28, 2000, the Attorney General, the Secretary of Homeland Security and the Secretary of State shall promulgate regulations for law enforcement personnel, immigration officials, and Department of State officials to implement the following:

(1) PROTECTIONS WHILE IN CUSTODY.—Victims of severe forms of trafficking, while in the custody of the Federal Government and to the extent practicable, shall—

(A) not be detained in facilities inappropriate to their status as crime victims;

(B) receive necessary medical care and other assistance; and

(C) be provided protection if a victim's safety is at risk or if there is danger of additional harm by recapture of the victim by a trafficker, including—

(i) taking measures to protect trafficked persons and their family members from intimidation and threats of reprisals and reprisals from traffickers and their associates; and

(ii) ensuring that the names and identifying information of trafficked persons and their family members are not disclosed to the public.

(2) ACCESS TO INFORMATION.—Victims of severe forms of trafficking shall have access to information about their rights and translation services. To the extent practicable, victims of severe forms of trafficking shall have access to information about federally funded or administered anti-trafficking programs that provide services to victims of severe forms of trafficking.

(3) AUTHORITY TO PERMIT CONTINUED PRESENCE IN THE UNITED STATES.—

(A) TRAFFICKING VICTIMS.—

(i) IN GENERAL.—If a Federal law enforcement official files an application stating that an alien is a victim of a severe form of trafficking and may be a potential witness to such trafficking, the Secretary of Homeland Security may permit the alien to remain in the United States to facilitate the investigation and prosecution of those responsible for such crime.

(ii) SAFETY.—While investigating and prosecuting suspected traffickers, Federal law enforcement officials described in clause (i) shall endeavor to make reasonable efforts to protect the safety of trafficking victims, including taking measures to protect trafficked persons and their family members from intimidation, threats of reprisals, and reprisals from traffickers and their associates.

(iii) CONTINUATION OF PRESENCE.—The Secretary shall permit an alien described in clause (i) who has filed a civil action under section 1595 of Title 18, to remain in the United States until such action is concluded. If the Secretary, in consultation with the Attorney General, determines that the alien has failed to exercise due diligence in pursuing such action, the Secretary may revoke the order permitting the alien to remain in the United States.

(iv) EXCEPTION.—Notwithstanding clause (iii), an alien described in such clause may be deported before the conclusion of the administrative and legal proceedings related to a complaint described in such clause if such alien is inadmissible under paragraph (2)(A)(i)(II), (2)(B), (2)(C), (2)(E), (2)(H), (2)(I), (3)(A)(i), (3)(A)(iii), (3)(B), or (3)(C) of section 1182(a) of Title 8.

(B) PAROLE FOR RELATIVES.—Law enforcement officials may submit written requests to the Secretary of Homeland Security, in accordance with section 1229b(b)(6) of this title, to permit the parole into the United States of certain relatives of an alien described in subparagraph (A)(i).

(C) STATE AND LOCAL LAW ENFORCEMENT.—The Secretary of Homeland Security, in consultation with the Attorney General, shall—

(i) develop materials to assist State and local law enforcement officials in working with Federal law enforcement to obtain continued presence for victims of a severe form of trafficking in cases investigated or prosecuted at the State or local level; and

(ii) distribute the materials developed under clause (i) to State and local law enforcement officials.

(4) TRAINING OF GOVERNMENT PERSONNEL.—Appropriate personnel of the Department of State, the Department of Homeland Security, the Department of Health and Human Services, *the Department of Labor, the Equal Employment Opportunity Commission,* and the Department of Justice shall be trained in identifying victims of severe forms of trafficking and providing for the protection of such victims, including juvenile victims. The Attorney General and the Secretary of Health and Human Services, *in consultation with the Secretary of Labor,* shall provide training to State and local officials to improve the identification and protection of such victims.

*   *   *   *   *   *   *

Historical and Statutory Notes

Establishment of Pilot Program for Residential Rehabilitative Facilities for Victims of Trafficking

Pub.L. 109–164, Title I, § 102(b), Jan. 10, 2006, 119 Stat. 3561, as amended Pub. L. 110–457, Title III, §§ 302(1), 304(b), Dec. 23, 2008, 122 Stat. 5087, provided that:
(1) STUDY.—

(A) IN GENERAL.—Not later than 180 days after the date of the enactment of this Act [Jan. 10, 2006], the Administrator of the United States Agency for International Development shall carry out a study to identify best practices for the rehabilitation of victims of trafficking in group residential facilities in foreign countries.

(B) FACTORS.—In carrying out the study under subparagraph (A), the Administrator shall—

(i) investigate factors relating to the rehabilitation of victims of trafficking in group residential facilities, such as the appropriate size of such facilities, services to be provided, length of stay, and cost; and

(ii) give consideration to ensure the safety and security of victims of trafficking, provide alternative sources of income for such victims, assess and provide for the educational needs of such victims, including literacy, and assess the psychological needs of such victims and provide professional counseling, as appropriate.

(2) PILOT PROGRAM.—Upon completion of the study carried out pursuant to paragraph (1), the Administrator of the United States Agency for International Development shall establish and carry out a pilot program to establish residential treatment facilities in foreign countries for victims of trafficking based upon the best practices identified in the study.

(3) PURPOSES.—The purposes of the pilot program established pursuant to paragraph (2) are to—

(A) provide benefits and services to victims of trafficking, including shelter, psychological counseling, and assistance in developing independent living skills;

(B) assess the benefits of providing residential treatment facilities for victims of trafficking, as well as the most efficient and cost-effective means of providing such facilities; and

(C) assess the need for and feasibility of establishing additional residential treatment facilities for victims of trafficking.

(4) SELECTION OF SITES.—The Administrator of the United States Agency for International Development shall select 2 sites at which to operate the pilot program established pursuant to paragraph (2).

(5) FORM OF ASSISTANCE.—In order to carry out the responsibilities of this subsection, the Administrator of the United States Agency for International Development shall enter into contracts with, or make grants to, organizations with relevant expertise in the delivery of services to victims of trafficking.

(6) REPORT.—Not later than one year after the date on which the first pilot program is established pursuant to paragraph (2), the Administrator of the United States Agency for International Development shall submit to the Committee on Foreign Affairs of the House of Representatives and the Committee on Foreign Relations of the Senate a report on the implementation of this subsection.

⟦(7) AUTHORIZATION OF APPROPRIATIONS.—There are authorized to be appropriated to the Administrator of the United States Agency for International Development to carry out this subsection $2,500,000 for each of the fiscal years 2008 through 2011.⟧

*   *   *   *   *   *   *

SEC. 7106. MINIMUM REQUIREMENTS FOR THE ELIMINATION OF TRAFFICKING.

(a) MINIMUM STANDARDS.—For purposes of this chapter, the minimum standards for the elimination of trafficking applicable to the government of a country of origin, transit, or destination for victims of severe forms of trafficking are the following:

(1) The government of the country should prohibit severe forms of trafficking in persons and punish acts of such trafficking.

(2) For the knowing commission of any act of sex trafficking involving force, fraud, coercion, or in which the victim of sex trafficking is a child incapable of giving meaningful consent, or of trafficking which includes rape or kidnapping or which causes a death, the government of the country should prescribe punishment commensurate with that for grave crimes, such as forcible sexual assault.

(3) For the knowing commission of any act of a severe form of trafficking in persons, the government of the country should prescribe punishment that is sufficiently stringent to deter and that adequately reflects the heinous nature of the offense.

(4) The government of the country should make serious and sustained efforts to eliminate severe forms of trafficking in persons.

(b) CRITERIA.—In determinations under subsection (a)(4) of this section, the following factors should be considered as indicia of serious and sustained efforts to eliminate severe forms of trafficking in persons:

(1) Whether the government of the country vigorously investigates and prosecutes acts of severe forms of trafficking in persons, and convicts and sentences persons responsible for such acts, that take place wholly or partly within the territory of the country, including, as appropriate, requiring incarceration of individuals convicted of such acts. For purposes of the preceding sentence, suspended or significantly-reduced sentences for convictions of principal actors in cases of severe forms of trafficking in persons shall be considered, on a case-by-case basis, whether to be considered an indicator of serious and sustained efforts to eliminate severe forms of trafficking in persons. After reasonable requests from the Department of State for data regarding investigations, prosecutions, convictions, and sentences, a government which does not provide such data, consistent with the capacity of such government to obtain such data, shall be presumed not to have vigorously investigated, prosecuted, convicted or sentenced such acts. During the periods prior to the annual report submitted on June 1, 2004, and on June 1, 2005, and the periods afterwards until September 30 of each such year, the Secretary of State may

disregard the presumption contained in the preceding sentence if the government has provided some data to the Department of State regarding such acts and the Secretary has determined that the government is making a good faith effort to collect such data.

(2) Whether the government of the country protects victims of severe forms of trafficking in persons and encourages their assistance in the investigation and prosecution of such trafficking, including provisions for legal alternatives to their removal to countries in which they would face retribution or hardship, and ensures that victims are not inappropriately incarcerated, fined, or otherwise penalized solely for unlawful acts as a direct result of being trafficked, including by providing training to law enforcement and immigration officials regarding the identification and treatment of trafficking victims using approaches that focus on the needs of the victims.

(3) Whether the government of the country has adopted measures to prevent severe forms of trafficking in persons, such as measures to inform and educate the public, including potential victims, about the causes and consequences of severe forms of trafficking in persons, measures to establish the identity of local populations, including birth registration, citizenship, and nationality, measures to ensure that its nationals who are deployed abroad as part of a [peacekeeping] *diplomatic, peacekeeping,* or other similar mission do not engage in or facilitate severe forms of trafficking in persons or exploit victims of such trafficking[, and measures], *a transparent system for remediating or punishing such public officials as a deterrent, measures* to prevent the use of forced labor or child labor in violation of international standards, *effective bilateral, multilateral, or regional information sharing and cooperation arrangements with source, transit, or destination countries in its trafficking route, and effective policies or laws regulating foreign labor recruiters and holding them civilly and criminally liable for fraudulent recruiting.*

(4) Whether the government of the country cooperates with other governments in the investigation and prosecution of severe forms of trafficking in persons *and has entered into bilateral, multilateral, or regional law enforcement cooperation and coordination arrangements with source, transit, and destination countries in its trafficking route.*

(5) Whether the government of the country extradites persons charged with acts of severe forms of trafficking in persons on substantially the same terms and to substantially the same extent as persons charged with other serious crimes (or, to the extent such extradition would be inconsistent with the laws of such country or with international agreements to which the country is a party, whether the government is taking all appropriate measures to modify or replace such laws and treaties so as to permit such extradition).

(6) Whether the government of the country monitors immigration and emigration patterns for evidence of severe forms of trafficking in persons and whether law enforcement agencies of the country respond to any such evidence in a manner that is

consistent with the vigorous investigation and prosecution of acts of such trafficking, as well as with the protection of human rights of victims and the internationally recognized human right to leave any country, including one's own, and to return to one's own country.

(7) Whether the government of the country vigorously investigates, prosecutes, convicts, and sentences public officials, *including diplomats and soldiers,* who participate in or facilitate severe forms of trafficking in persons, including nationals of the country who are deployed abroad as part of a [peacekeeping] *diplomatic, peacekeeping,* or other similar mission who engage in or facilitate severe forms of trafficking in persons or exploit victims of such trafficking, and takes all appropriate measures against officials who condone such trafficking. *A government's failure to appropriately address public allegations against such public officials, especially once such officials have returned to their home countries, shall be considered inaction under these criteria.* After reasonable requests from the Department of State for data regarding such investigations, prosecutions, convictions, and sentences, a government which does not provide such data consistent with its resources shall be presumed not to have vigorously investigated, prosecuted, convicted, or sentenced such acts. During the periods prior to the annual report submitted on June 1, 2004, and on June 1, 2005, and the periods afterwards until September 30 of each such year, the Secretary of State may disregard the presumption contained in the preceding sentence if the government has provided some data to the Department of State regarding such acts and the Secretary has determined that the government is making a good faith effort to collect such data.

(8) Whether the percentage of victims of severe forms of trafficking in the country that are non-citizens of such countries is insignificant.

(9) Whether the government has entered into transparent partnerships, cooperative arrangements, or agreements with—

> *(A) domestic civil society organizations or the private sector to assist the government's efforts to prevent trafficking, protect victims, and punish traffickers; or*
> *(B) the United States toward agreed goals and objectives in the collective fight against trafficking.*

[(9)] *(10)* Whether the government of the country, consistent with the capacity of such government, systematically monitors its efforts to satisfy the criteria described in paragraphs (1) through (8) and makes available publicly a periodic assessment of such efforts.

[(10)] *(11)* Whether the government of the country achieves appreciable progress in eliminating severe forms of trafficking when compared to the assessment in the previous year.

[(11)] *(12)* Whether the government of the country has made serious and sustained efforts to reduce the demand for—

> (A) commercial sex acts; and
> (B) participation in international sex tourism by nationals of the country.

SEC. 7107. ACTIONS AGAINST GOVERNMENTS FAILING TO MEET MINIMUM STANDARDS.

(a) STATEMENT OF POLICY.—It is the policy of the United States not to provide nonhumanitarian, nontrade-related foreign assistance to any government that—

(1) does not comply with minimum standards for the elimination of trafficking; and

(2) is not making significant efforts to bring itself into compliance with such standards.

(b) REPORTS TO CONGRESS.—

(1) ANNUAL REPORT.—Not later than June 1 of each year, the Secretary of State shall submit to the appropriate congressional committees a report [with respect to the status of severe forms of trafficking in persons that shall include—] *describing the anti-trafficking efforts of governments according to the minimum standards and criteria enumerated in section 7106, and the nature and scope of trafficking in persons in each country and analysis of the trend lines for individual governmental efforts. The report should include*—

(A) a list of those countries, if any, to which the minimum standards for the elimination of trafficking are applicable and whose governments fully comply with such standards;

(B) a list of those countries, if any, to which the minimum standards for the elimination of trafficking are applicable and whose governments do not yet fully comply with such standards but are making significant efforts to bring themselves into [compliance;] *compliance, including the identification and mention of governments that*—

(i) are on such list and have demonstrated exemplary progress in their efforts to reach the minimum standards; or

(ii) have committed to the Secretary to accomplish certain actions before the subsequent year's annual report in an attempt to reach full compliance with the minimum standards;

(C) a list of those countries, if any, to which the minimum standards for the elimination of trafficking are applicable and whose governments do not fully comply with such standards and are not making significant efforts to bring themselves into compliance;

(D) information on the measures taken by the United Nations, the Organization for Security and Cooperation in Europe, the North Atlantic Treaty Organization and, as appropriate, other multilateral organizations in which the United States participates, to prevent the involvement of the organization's employees, contractor personnel, and peacekeeping forces in trafficking in persons or the exploitation of victims of trafficking;

(E) reporting and analysis on the emergence or shifting of global patterns in human trafficking, including data on the number of victims trafficked to, through, or from major source and destination countries, disaggregated by nationality, gender, and age, to the extent possible[; and]*;*

(F) emerging issues in human trafficking[.]; and

(G) a section entitled "Exemplary Governments and Practices in the Eradication of Trafficking in Persons" to highlight—

> *(i) effective practices and use of innovation and technology in prevention, protection, prosecution, and partnerships, including by foreign governments, the private sector, and domestic civil society actors; and*

> *(ii) governments that have shown exemplary overall efforts to combat trafficking in persons.*

[(2) INTERIM REPORTS.—In addition to the annual report under paragraph (1), the Secretary of State may submit to the appropriate congressional committees at any time one or more interim reports with respect to the status of severe forms of trafficking in persons, including information about countries whose governments—

[(A) have come into or out of compliance with the minimum standards for the elimination of trafficking; or

[(B) have begun or ceased to make significant efforts to bring themselves into compliance, since the transmission of the last annual report.]

[(3)] *(2)* SPECIAL WATCH LIST.—

(A) SUBMISSION OF LIST.—Not later than the date on which the determinations described in subsections (c) and (d) of this section are submitted to the appropriate congressional committees in accordance with such subsections, the Secretary of State shall submit to the appropriate congressional committees a list of countries that the Secretary determines requires special scrutiny during the following year. The list shall be composed of the following countries:

> (i) Countries that have been listed pursuant to paragraph (1)(A) in the current annual report and were listed pursuant to paragraph (1)(B) in the previous annual report.

> (ii) Countries that have been listed pursuant to paragraph (1)(B) pursuant to the current annual report and were listed pursuant to paragraph (1)(C) in the previous annual report.

> (iii) Countries that have been listed pursuant to paragraph (1)(B) pursuant to the current annual report, where—

>> (I) the absolute number of victims of severe forms of trafficking is very significant or is significantly increasing;

>> (II) there is a failure to provide evidence of increasing efforts to combat severe forms of trafficking in persons from the previous year, including increased investigations, prosecutions and convictions of trafficking crimes, increased assistance to victims, and decreasing evidence of complicity in severe forms of trafficking by government officials; or

>> (III) the determination that a country is making significant efforts to bring themselves into compli-

ance with minimum standards was based on commitments by the country to take additional future steps over the next year.

(B) INTERIM ASSESSMENT.—Not later than February 1st of each year, the Secretary of State shall provide to the appropriate congressional committees an assessment of the progress that each country on the special watch list described in subparagraph (A) has made since the last annual report.

(C) RELATION OF SPECIAL WATCH LIST TO ANNUAL TRAFFICKING IN PERSONS REPORT.—A determination that a country shall not be placed on the special watch list described in subparagraph (A) shall not affect in any way the determination to be made in the following year as to whether a country is complying with the minimum standards for the elimination of trafficking or whether a country is making significant efforts to bring itself into compliance with such standards.

(D) COUNTRIES ON SPECIAL WATCH LIST FOR 2 CONSECUTIVE YEARS.—

(i) IN GENERAL.—Except as provided under clause (ii), a country that is included on the special watch list described in subparagraph (A) for 2 consecutive years after December 23, 2008, shall be included on the list of countries described in paragraph (1)(C).

(ii) EXERCISE OF WAIVER AUTHORITY.—The President may waive the application of clause (i) for up to 2 years if the President determines, and reports credible evidence to the Committee on Foreign Relations of the Senate and the Committee on Foreign Affairs of the House of Representatives, that such a waiver is justified because—

(I) the country has a written plan to begin making significant efforts to bring itself into compliance with the minimum standards for the elimination of trafficking;

(II) the plan, if implemented, would constitute making such significant efforts; and

(III) the country is devoting sufficient resources to implement the plan.

(E) PUBLIC NOTICE.—Not later than 30 days after notifying Congress of each country determined to have met the requirements under subclauses (I) through (III) of subparagraph (D)(ii), the Secretary of State shall provide a detailed description of the credible evidence supporting such determination on a publicly available website maintained by the Department of State.

[(4)] *(3)* SIGNIFICANT EFFORTS.—In determinations under paragraph (1) or (2) as to whether the government of a country is making significant efforts to bring itself into compliance with the minimum standards for the elimination of trafficking, the Secretary of State shall consider—

(A) the extent to which the country is a country of origin, transit, or destination for severe forms of trafficking;

(B) the extent of noncompliance with the minimum standards by the government and, particularly, the extent to which officials or employees of the government have participated in, facilitated, condoned, or are otherwise complicit in severe forms of trafficking; and

(C) what measures are reasonable to bring the government into compliance with the minimum standards in light of the resources and capabilities of the government.

(c) NOTIFICATION.—Not less than 45 days or more than 90 days after the submission, on or after January 1, 2003, of an annual report under subsection (b)(1) of this section, or an interim report under subsection (b)(2) of this section, the President shall submit to the appropriate congressional committees a notification of one of the determinations listed in subsection (d) of this section with respect to each foreign country whose government, according to such report—

(1) does not comply with the minimum standards for the elimination of trafficking; and

(2) is not making significant efforts to bring itself into compliance, as described in subsection (b)(1)(C) of this section.

(d) PRESIDENTIAL DETERMINATIONS.—The determinations referred to in subsection (c) of this section are the following:

(1) WITHHOLDING OF NONHUMANITARIAN, NONTRADE-RELATED ASSISTANCE.—The President has determined that—

(A)(i) the United States will not provide nonhumanitarian, nontrade-related foreign assistance to the government of the country for the subsequent fiscal year until such government complies with the minimum standards or makes significant efforts to bring itself into compliance; or

(ii) in the case of a country whose government received no nonhumanitarian, nontrade-related foreign assistance from the United States during the previous fiscal year, the United States will not provide such assistance to the government of the country for the subsequent fiscal year and will not provide funding for participation by officials or employees of such governments in educational and cultural exchange programs for the subsequent fiscal year until such government complies with the minimum standards or makes significant efforts to bring itself into compliance; and

(B) the President will instruct the United States Executive Director of each multilateral development bank and of the International Monetary Fund to vote against, and to use the Executive Director's best efforts to deny, any loan or other utilization of the funds of the respective institution to that country (other than for humanitarian assistance, for trade-related assistance, or for development assistance which directly addresses basic human needs, is not administered by the government of the sanctioned country, and confers no benefit to that government) for the subsequent fiscal year until such government complies with the minimum standards or makes significant efforts to bring itself into compliance.

(2) ONGOING, MULTIPLE, BROAD-BASED RESTRICTIONS ON ASSISTANCE IN RESPONSE TO HUMAN RIGHTS VIOLATIONS.—The President has determined that such country is already subject to multiple, broad-based restrictions on assistance imposed in significant part in response to human rights abuses and such restrictions are ongoing and are comparable to the restrictions provided in paragraph (1). Such determination shall be accompanied by a description of the specific restriction or restrictions that were the basis for making such determination.

(3) SUBSEQUENT COMPLIANCE.—The Secretary of State has determined that the government of the country has come into compliance with the minimum standards or is making significant efforts to bring itself into compliance.

(4) CONTINUATION OF ASSISTANCE IN THE NATIONAL INTEREST.—Notwithstanding the failure of the government of the country to comply with minimum standards for the elimination of trafficking and to make significant efforts to bring itself into compliance, the President has determined that the provision to the country of nonhumanitarian, nontrade-related foreign assistance or funding for participation in educational and cultural exchange programs, or the multilateral assistance described in paragraph (1)(B), or both, would promote the purposes of this chapter or is otherwise in the national interest of the United States.

(5) EXERCISE OF WAIVER AUTHORITY.—

(A) IN GENERAL.—The President may exercise the authority under paragraph (4) with respect to—

(i) all nonhumanitarian, nontrade-related foreign assistance or funding for participation in educational and cultural exchange programs to a country;

(ii) all multilateral assistance described in paragraph (1)(B) to a country; or

(iii) one or more programs, projects, or activities of such assistance.

(B) AVOIDANCE OF SIGNIFICANT ADVERSE EFFECTS.—The President shall exercise the authority under paragraph (4) when necessary to avoid significant adverse effects on vulnerable populations, including women and children.

(6) DEFINITION OF MULTILATERAL DEVELOPMENT BANK.—In this subsection, the term "multilateral development bank" refers to any of the following institutions: the International Bank for Reconstruction and Development, the International Development Association, the International Finance Corporation, the Inter-American Development Bank, the Asian Development Bank, the Inter-American Investment Corporation, the African Development Bank, the African Development Fund, the European Bank for Reconstruction and Development, and the Multilateral Investment Guaranty Agency.

(e) CERTIFICATION.—Together with any notification under subsection (c) of this section, the President shall provide a certification by the Secretary of State that, with respect to any assistance described in clause (ii), (iii), or (v) of [section 7102(7)(A)] *section 7102(8)(A)* of this title, or with respect to any assistance described in [section 7102(7)(B)] *section 7102(8)(B)* of this title, no assistance is intended to be received or used by any agency or official who has participated in, facilitated, or condoned a severe form of trafficking in persons.

(f) After the President has made a determination described in subsection (d)(1) of this section with respect to the government of a country, the President may at any time make a determination described in paragraphs (4) and (5) of subsection (d) of this section to waive, in whole or in part, the measures imposed against the country by the previous determination under subsection (d)(1) of this section.

* * * * * * *

SEC. 7109a. RESEARCH ON DOMESTIC AND INTERNATIONAL TRAFFICKING IN PERSONS.

* * * * * * *

(b) ROLE OF HUMAN SMUGGLING AND TRAFFICKING CENTER.—

(1) IN GENERAL.—The research initiatives described in paragraphs (4) and (5) of subsection (a) shall be carried out by the Human Smuggling and Trafficking Center, established under section 1777 of Title 8.

(2) DATABASE.—The database described in subsection (a)(5) shall be established by combining all applicable data collected by each Federal department and agency represented on the Interagency Task Force to Monitor and Combat Trafficking, consistent with the protection of sources and methods, and, to the maximum extent practicable, applicable data from relevant international organizations, to—

(A) improve the coordination of the collection of data related to trafficking in persons by each agency of the United States Government that collects such data;

(B) promote uniformity of such data collection and standards and systems related to such collection;

(C) undertake a meta-analysis of patterns of trafficking in persons, slavery, and slave-like conditions to develop and analyze global trends in human trafficking;

(D) identify emerging issues in human trafficking and establishing integrated methods to combat them; and

(E) identify research priorities to respond to global patterns and emerging issues.

(3) CONSULTATION.—The database established in accordance with paragraph (2) shall be maintained in consultation with the Director of the Office to Monitor and Combat Trafficking in Persons of the Department of State.

(4) AUTHORIZATION OF APPROPRIATIONS.—There are authorized to be appropriated [$2,000,000] *$1,000,000* to the Human Smuggling and Trafficking Center for each of the fiscal years [2008 through 2011] *2012 through 2015* to carry out the activities described in this subsection.

* * * * * * *

SEC. 7109B. PRESIDENTIAL AWARD FOR EXTRAORDINARY EFFORTS *AND TECHNOLOGICAL INNOVATIONS* TO COMBAT TRAFFICKING IN PERSONS.

(a) ESTABLISHMENT OF AWARD.—The President is authorized to establish an award, to be known as the "Presidential Award for Extraordinary Efforts *and technological innovations* To Combat Trafficking in Persons", for extraordinary efforts to combat trafficking in persons. To the maximum extent practicable, the Secretary of State shall present the award annually to not more than 5 individuals or organizations, including—

(1) individuals who are United States citizens or foreign nationals; [and]

(2) United States or foreign nongovernmental organizations[.];

(3) private sector entities; and

(4) national governments or regional and local governmental units.

(b) SELECTION.—The President shall establish procedures for selecting recipients of the award authorized under subsection (a).

(c) CEREMONY.—The Secretary of State shall host an annual ceremony for recipients of the award authorized under subsection (a) as soon as practicable after the date on which the Secretary submits to Congress the report required under section 7107(b)(1) of this title. The Secretary of State may pay the travel costs of each recipient and a guest of each recipient who attends the ceremony.

(d) AUTHORIZATION OF APPROPRIATIONS.—There are authorized to be appropriated, for each of the fiscal years 2008 through 2011, such sums as may be necessary to carry out this section.

* * * * * * *

SEC. 7110. AUTHORIZATIONS OF APPROPRIATIONS.

* * * * * * *

(a) AUTHORIZATION OF APPROPRIATIONS IN SUPPORT OF THE TASK FORCE.—To carry out the purposes of sections 7103(e), 7103(f) and 7107 of this title, there are authorized to be appropriated to the Secretary of State [$5,500,000 for each of the fiscal years 2008 through 2011] *$2,000,000 for each of the fiscal years 2012 through 2015.* In addition, there are authorized to be appropriated to the Office to Monitor and Combat Trafficking $1,500,000 for additional personnel, *including regional trafficking in persons officers,* for each of the fiscal years 2008 through 2011[, and $3,000 for official reception and representation expenses for each of the fiscal years 2008 through 2011].

(b) AUTHORIZATION OF APPROPRIATIONS TO THE SECRETARY OF HEALTH AND HUMAN SERVICES.—

(1) ELIGIBILITY FOR BENEFITS AND ASSISTANCE.—To carry out the purposes of section 7105(b) of this title, there are authorized to be appropriated to the Secretary of Health and Human Services [$12,500,000 for each of the fiscal years 2008 through 2011] *$14,500,000 for each of the fiscal years 2012 through 2015.*

(2) ADDITIONAL BENEFITS FOR TRAFFICKING VICTIMS.—To carry out the purposes of section 7105(f) of this title, there are authorized to be appropriated [to the Secretary of Health and

Human Services—] *$8,000,000 to the Secretary of Health and Human Services for each of the fiscal years 2012 through 2015.*
  [(A) $2,500,000 for fiscal year 2008;
  [(B) $5,000,000 for fiscal year 2009;
  [(C) $7,000,000 for fiscal year 2010; and
  [(D) $7,000,000 for fiscal year 2011.]
(c) AUTHORIZATION OF APPROPRIATIONS TO THE SECRETARY OF STATE.—
    (1) BILATERAL ASSISTANCE TO COMBAT TRAFFICKING.—
      (A) PREVENTION.—To carry out the purposes of section 7104 of this title, there are authorized to be appropriated to the Secretary of State $10,000,000 for each of the fiscal years [2008 through 2011] *2012 through 2015.*
      (B) PROTECTION.—To carry out the purposes of section 7105(a) of this title, there are authorized to be appropriated to the Secretary of State [$15,000,000 for fiscal year 2003 and $10,000,000 for each of the fiscal years 2008 through 2011] *$10,000,000 for each of the fiscal years 2012 through 2015.* To carry out the purposes of section 7105(a)(1)(F) of this title, there are authorized to be appropriated to the Secretary of State $1,000,000 for each of the fiscal years [2008 through 2011] *2012 through 2015.*
      (C) PROSECUTION AND MEETING MINIMUM STANDARDS.— To carry out the purposes of section 2152d of this title, there are authorized to be appropriated $10,000,000 for each of the fiscal years [2008 through 2011] *2012 through 2015* to assist in promoting prosecution of traffickers and otherwise to assist countries in meeting the minimum standards described in section 7106 of this title, including $250,000 for each such fiscal year to carry out training activities for law enforcement officers, prosecutors, and members of the judiciary with respect to trafficking in persons at the International Law Enforcement Academies.
    (2) PREPARATION OF ANNUAL COUNTRY REPORTS ON HUMAN RIGHTS.—To carry out the purposes of sections 2151n(f) and 2304(h) of this title, there are authorized to be appropriated to the Secretary of State such sums as may be necessary to include the additional information required by that section in the annual Country Reports on Human Rights Practices.
(d) AUTHORIZATION OF APPROPRIATIONS TO ATTORNEY GENERAL.—
    [(A)] *(1)* ELIGIBILITY FOR BENEFITS AND ASSISTANCE.—To carry out the purposes of section 7105(b) of this title, there are authorized to be appropriated to the Attorney General [$10,000,000 for each of the fiscal years 2008 through 2011] *$11,000,000 for each of the fiscal years 2012 through 2015.*
    [(B)] *(2)* ASSISTANCE TO FOREIGN COUNTRIES.—To carry out the purposes of section 2152d of this title, there are authorized to be appropriated to the President, acting through the Attorney General and the Secretary of State, $250,000 for each of fiscal years 2008 through 2011 to carry out training activities for law enforcement officers, prosecutors, and members of the

judiciary with respect to trafficking in persons at the International Law Enforcement Academies.

[(C)] *(3)* ADDITIONAL BENEFITS FOR TRAFFICKING VICTIMS.—To carry out the purposes of section 7105(f) of this title, there are authorized to be appropriated [to the Attorney General—] *$11,000,000 to the Attorney General for each of the fiscal years 2012 through 2015.*

[(i) $2,500,000 for fiscal year 2008;
[(ii) $5,000,000 for fiscal year 2009;
[(iii) $7,000,000 for fiscal year 2010; and
[(iv) $7,000,000 for fiscal year 2011.]

(e) AUTHORIZATION OF APPROPRIATIONS TO PRESIDENT.—

(1) FOREIGN VICTIM ASSISTANCE.—To carry out the purposes of section 7104 of this title, there are authorized to be appropriated to the President [$15,000,000 for each of the fiscal years 2008 through 2011] *$7,500,000 for each of the fiscal years 2012 through 2015.*

(2) ASSISTANCE TO FOREIGN COUNTRIES TO MEET MINIMUM STANDARDS.—To carry out the purposes of section 2152d of this title, there are authorized to be appropriated to the President [$15,000,000 for each of the fiscal years 2008 through 2011] *$7,500,000 for each of the fiscal years 2012 through 2015.*

(3) RESEARCH.—To carry out the purposes of section 7109a of this title, there are authorized to be appropriated to the President $2,000,000 for each of the fiscal years 2008 through 2011.

(f) AUTHORIZATION OF APPROPRIATIONS TO THE SECRETARY OF LABOR.—To carry out the purposes of section 7105(b) of this title, there are authorized to be appropriated to the Secretary of Labor [$10,000,000 for each of the fiscal years 2008 through 2011] *$5,000,000 for each of the fiscal years 2012 through 2015.*

(g) LIMITATION ON USE OF FUNDS.—

(1) RESTRICTION ON PROGRAMS.—No funds made available to carry out this chapter, or any amendment made by this chapter, may be used to promote, support, or advocate the legalization or practice of prostitution. Nothing in the preceding sentence shall be construed to preclude assistance designed to promote the purposes of this Act by ameliorating the suffering of, or health risks to, victims while they are being trafficked or after they are out of the situation that resulted from such victims being trafficked.

(2) RESTRICTION ON ORGANIZATIONS.—No funds made available to carry out this chapter, or any amendment made by this division, may be used to implement any program that targets victims of severe forms of trafficking in persons described in [section 7102(8)(A)] *section 7102(9)(A)* of this title through any organization that has not stated in either a grant application, a grant agreement, or both, that it does not promote, support, or advocate the legalization or practice of prostitution. The preceding sentence shall not apply to organizations that provide services to individuals solely after they are no longer engaged in activities that resulted from such victims being trafficked.

(h) AUTHORIZATION OF APPROPRIATIONS TO DIRECTOR OF THE FBI.—There are authorized to be appropriated to the Director of the Federal Bureau of Investigation $15,000,000 for each of the fiscal years 2008 through 2011, to remain available until expended, to investigate severe forms of trafficking in persons.

(i) AUTHORIZATION OF APPROPRIATIONS TO THE SECRETARY OF HOMELAND SECURITY.—There are authorized to be appropriated to the Secretary of Homeland Security, [$18,000,000 for each of the fiscal years 2008 through 2011] *$10,000,000 for each of the fiscal years 2012 through 2015,* to remain available until expended, for investigations by the Bureau of Immigration and Customs Enforcement of severe forms of trafficking in persons.

* * * * * * *

SEC. 7112. ADDITIONAL ACTIVITIES TO MONITOR AND COMBAT FORCED LABOR AND CHILD LABOR.

(a) ACTIVITIES OF THE DEPARTMENT OF STATE.—

(1) FINDING.—Congress finds that in the report submitted to Congress by the Secretary of State in June 2005 pursuant to section 7107(b) of this title, the list of countries whose governments do not comply with the minimum standards for the elimination of trafficking and are not making significant efforts to bring themselves into compliance was composed of a large number of countries in which the trafficking involved forced labor, including the trafficking of women into domestic servitude.

(2) SENSE OF CONGRESS.—It is the sense of Congress that the Director of the Office to Monitor and Combat Trafficking of the Department of State should intensify the focus of the Office on forced labor in the countries described in paragraph (1) and other countries in which forced labor continues to be a serious human rights concern.

(3) INFORMATION SHARING.—The Secretary of State shall, on a regular basis, provide information relating to child labor and forced labor in the production of goods in violation of international standards to the Department of Labor to be used in developing the list described in subsection (b)(2)(C).

(b) ACTIVITIES OF THE DEPARTMENT OF LABOR.—

(1) IN GENERAL.—The Secretary of Labor, acting through the head of the Bureau of International Labor Affairs of the Department of Labor, shall carry out additional activities to monitor and combat forced labor and child labor in foreign countries as described in paragraph (2).

(2) ADDITIONAL ACTIVITIES DESCRIBED.—The additional activities referred to in paragraph (1) are—

(A) to monitor the use of forced labor and child labor in violation of international standards;

(B) to provide information regarding trafficking in persons for the purpose of forced labor to the Office to Monitor and Combat Trafficking of the Department of State for inclusion in trafficking in persons report required by section 7107(b) of this title;

(C) to develop and make available to the public a list of goods from countries that the Bureau of International Labor Affairs has reason to believe are produced by forced labor or child labor in violation of international standards;

(D) to work with persons who are involved in the production of goods on the list described in subparagraph (C) to create a standard set of practices that will reduce the likelihood that such persons will produce goods using the labor described in such subparagraph; and

(E) to consult with other departments and agencies of the United States Government to reduce forced and child labor internationally and ensure that products made by forced labor and child labor in violation of international standards are not imported into the United States.

(3) SUBMISSION TO CONGRESS.—Not later than December 1, 2012, and every 2 years thereafter, the Secretary of Labor shall submit the list developed under paragraph (2)(C) to Congress.

*　　*　　*　　*　　*　　*　　*

CHAPTER 85—NORTH KOREAN HUMAN RIGHTS

*　　*　　*　　*　　*　　*　　*

SEC. 7833. ASSISTANCE PROVIDED OUTSIDE NORTH KOREA.

(a) ASSISTANCE.—The President is authorized to provide assistance to support organizations or persons that provide humanitarian assistance to North Koreans who are outside of North Korea without the permission of the Government of North Korea.

(b) TYPES OF ASSISTANCE.—Assistance provided under subsection (a) of this section should be used to provide—

(1) humanitarian assistance to North Korean refugees, defectors, migrants, and orphans outside of North Korea, which may include support for refugee camps or temporary settlements; and

(2) humanitarian assistance to North Korean women outside of North Korea who are victims of trafficking, as defined in [section 7102(14)] *section 7102(15)* of this title, or are in danger of being trafficked.

(c) AUTHORIZATION OF APPROPRIATIONS.—

(1) IN GENERAL.—In addition to funds otherwise available for such purposes, there are authorized to be appropriated to the President $20,000,000 for each of the fiscal years 2005 through 2012 to carry out this section.

(2) AVAILABILITY.—Amounts appropriated pursuant to the authorization of appropriations under paragraph (1) are authorized to remain available until expended.

*　　*　　*　　*　　*　　*　　*

TITLE 42—THE PUBLIC HEALTH AND WELFARE

*　　*　　*　　*　　*　　*　　*

CHAPTER 136—VIOLENT CRIME CONTROL AND LAW ENFORCEMENT

*　　*　　*　　*　　*　　*　　*

SEC. 14044. PREVENTION OF DOMESTIC TRAFFICKING IN PERSONS.

*　　*　　*　　*　　*　　*　　*

(c) AUTHORIZATION OF APPROPRIATIONS.—There are authorized to be appropriated—

(1) $1,500,000 for each of the fiscal years 2008 through 2011 to carry out the activities described in subsection (a)(1)(B)(i) and $1,500,000 for each of the fiscal years 2008 through 2011 to carry out the activities described in subsection (a)(1)(B)(ii); and

(2) [$1,000,000 for each of the fiscal years 2008 through 2011] *$250,000 for each of the fiscal years 2012 through 2015* to carry out the activities described in subsection (a)(2).

* * * * * * *

[SEC. 14044a. ESTABLISHMENT OF A GRANT PROGRAM TO DEVELOP, EXPAND, AND STRENGTHEN ASSISTANCE PROGRAMS FOR CERTAIN PERSONS SUBJECT TO TRAFFICKING.

[(a) GRANT PROGRAM.—The Secretary of Health and Human Services may make grants to States, Indian tribes, units of local government, and nonprofit, nongovernmental victims' service organizations to establish, develop, expand, and strengthen assistance programs for United States citizens or aliens admitted for permanent residence who are the subject of sex trafficking or severe forms of trafficking in persons that occurs, in whole or in part, within the territorial jurisdiction of the United States.

[(b) SELECTION FACTOR.—In selecting among applicants for grants under subsection (a) of this section, the Secretary shall give priority to applicants with experience in the delivery of services to persons who have been subjected to sexual abuse or commercial sexual exploitation and to applicants who would employ survivors of sexual abuse or commercial sexual exploitation as a part of their proposed project.

[(c) LIMITATION ON FEDERAL SHARE.—The Federal share of a grant made under this section may not exceed 75 percent of the total costs of the projects described in the application submitted.

[(d) AUTHORIZATION OF APPROPRIATIONS.—There are authorized to be appropriated $8,000,000 for each of the fiscal years 2008 through 2011 to carry out the activities described in this section.]

SEC. 14404a. ESTABLISHMENT OF A GRANT PROGRAM TO DEVELOP, EXPAND, AND STRENGTHEN ASSISTANCE PROGRAMS FOR CERTAIN PERSONS SUBJECT TO TRAFFICKING.

(a) DEFINITIONS.—In this section:

(1) ASSISTANT SECRETARY—The term 'Assistant Secretary' means the Assistant Secretary for Children and Families of the Department of Health and Human Services.

(2) ASSISTANT ATTORNEY GENERAL.—The term 'Assistant Attorney General' means the Assistant Attorney General for the Office of Justice Programs of the Department of Justice.

(3) ELIGIBLE ENTITY.—The term 'eligible entity' means a State or unit of local government that—

(A) has significant criminal activity involving sex trafficking of minors;

(B) has demonstrated cooperation between Federal, State, local, and, where applicable, tribal law enforcement agencies, prosecutors, and social service providers in addressing sex trafficking of minors;

(C) has developed a workable, multi-disciplinary plan to combat sex trafficking of minors, including—

(i) building or establishing a residential care facility for minor victims of sex trafficking;

(ii) the provision of rehabilitative care to minor victims of sex trafficking;

(iii) the provision of specialized training for law enforcement officers and social service providers for all forms of sex trafficking, with a focus on sex trafficking of minors;

(iv) prevention, deterrence, and prosecution of offenses involving sex trafficking of minors;

(v) cooperation or referral agreements with organizations providing outreach or other related services to runaway and homeless youth; and

(vi) law enforcement protocols or procedures to screen all individuals arrested for prostitution, whether adult or minor, for victimization by sex trafficking and by other crimes, such as sexual assault and domestic violence; and

(D) provides assurance that a minor victim of sex trafficking shall not be required to collaborate with law enforcement to have access to residential care or services provided with a grant under this section.

(4) MINOR VICTIM OF SEX TRAFFICKING.—The term 'minor victim of sex trafficking' means an individual who—

(A) is younger than 18 years of age, and is a victim of an offense described in section 1591(a) of title 18, United States Code, or a comparable State law; or

(B)(i) is not younger than 18 years of age nor older than 20 years of age;

(ii) before the individual reached 18 years of age, was described in subparagraph (A); and

(iii) was receiving shelter or services as a minor victim of sex trafficking.

(5) QUALIFIED NONGOVERNMENTAL ORGANIZATION.—The term "qualified nongovernmental organization" means an organization that—

(A) is not a State or unit of local government, or an agency of a State or unit of local government;

(B) has demonstrated experience providing services to victims of sex trafficking or related populations (such as runaway and homeless youth), or employs staff specialized in the treatment of sex trafficking victims; and

(C) demonstrates a plan to sustain the provision of services beyond the period of a grant awarded under this section.

(6) SEX TRAFFICKING OF A MINOR.—The term "sex trafficking of a minor" means an offense described in section 1591(a) of title 18, United States Code, or a comparable State law, against a minor.

(b) SEX TRAFFICKING BLOCK GRANTS.—

(1) GRANTS AUTHORIZED.—

(A) IN GENERAL.—The Assistant Attorney General, in consultation with the Assistant Secretary, may make block grants to 4 eligible entities located in different regions of the United States to combat sex trafficking of minors.

(B) REQUIREMENT.—Not fewer than 1 of the block grants made under subparagraph (A) shall be awarded to an eligible entity with a State population of less than 5,000,000.

(C) GRANT AMOUNT.—Subject to the availability of appropriations under subsection (g) to carry out this section, each grant made under this section shall be for an amount not less than $1,500,000 and not greater than $2,000,000.

(D) DURATION.—

(i) IN GENERAL.—A grant made under this section shall be for a period of 1 year.

(ii) RENEWAL.—

(I) IN GENERAL.—The Assistant Attorney General may renew a grant under this section for up to 3 1-year periods.

(II) PRIORITY.—In making grants in any fiscal year after the first fiscal year in which grants are made under this section, the Assistant Attorney General shall give priority to an eligible entity that received a grant in the preceding fiscal year and is eligible for renewal under this subparagraph, taking into account any evaluation of the eligible entity conducted under paragraph (4), if available.

(E) CONSULTATION.—In carrying out this section, the Assistant Attorney General shall consult with the Assistant Secretary with respect to—

(i) evaluations of grant recipients under paragraph (4);

(ii) avoiding unintentional duplication of grants; and

(iii) any other areas of shared concern.

(2) USE OF FUNDS.—

(A) ALLOCATION.—Not less than 67 percent of each grant made under paragraph (1) shall be used by the eligible entity to provide residential care and services (as described in clauses (i) through (iv) of subparagraph (B)) to minor victims of sex trafficking through qualified nongovernmental organizations.

(B) AUTHORIZED ACTIVITIES.—Grants awarded pursuant to paragraph (2) may be used for—

(i) providing residential care to minor victims of sex trafficking, including temporary or long-term placement as appropriate;

(ii) providing 24-hour emergency social services response for minor victims of sex trafficking;

(iii) providing minor victims of sex trafficking with clothing and other daily necessities needed to keep such victims from returning to living on the street;

(iv) case management services for minor victims of sex trafficking;

(v) mental health counseling for minor victims of sex trafficking, including specialized counseling and substance abuse treatment;

(vi) legal services for minor victims of sex trafficking;

(vii) specialized training for social service providers, public sector personnel, and private sector personnel likely to encounter sex trafficking victims on issues related to the sex trafficking of minors and severe forms of trafficking in persons;

(viii) outreach and education programs to provide information about deterrence and prevention of sex trafficking of minors;

(ix) programs to provide treatment to individuals charged or cited with purchasing or attempting to purchase sex acts in cases where—

(I) a treatment program can be mandated as a condition of a sentence, fine, suspended sentence, or probation, or is an appropriate alternative to criminal prosecution; and

(II) the individual was not charged with purchasing or attempting to purchase sex acts with a minor; and

(x) screening and referral of minor victims of severe forms of trafficking in persons.

(3) APPLICATION.—

(A) IN GENERAL.—Each eligible entity desiring a grant under this section shall submit an application to the Assistant Attorney General at such time, in such manner, and accompanied by such information as the Assistant Attorney General may reasonably require.

(B) CONTENTS.—Each application submitted pursuant to subparagraph (A) shall—

(i) describe the activities for which assistance under this section is sought; and

(ii) provide such additional assurances as the Assistant Attorney General determines to be essential to ensure compliance with the requirements of this section.

(4) EVALUATION.—The Assistant Attorney General shall enter into a contract with an academic or non-profit organization that has experience in issues related to sex trafficking of minors and evaluation of grant programs to conduct an annual evaluation of each grant made under this section to determine the impact and effectiveness of programs funded with the grant.

(c) MANDATORY EXCLUSION.—An eligible entity that receives a grant under this section that is found to have utilized grant funds for any unauthorized expenditure or otherwise unallowable cost shall not be eligible for any grant funds awarded under the grant for 2 fiscal years following the year in which the unauthorized expenditure or unallowable cost is reported.

(d) COMPLIANCE REQUIREMENT.—An eligible entity shall not be eligible to receive a grant under this section if, during the 5 fiscal years before the eligible entity submits an application for the grant, the eligible entity has been found to have violated the terms or con-

ditions of a Government grant program by utilizing grant funds for unauthorized expenditures or otherwise unallowable costs.

(e) ADMINISTRATIVE CAP.—The cost of administering the grants authorized by this section shall not exceed 3 percent of the total amount appropriated to carry out this section.

(f) AUDIT REQUIREMENT.—For fiscal years 2014 and 2015, the Inspector General of the Department of Justice shall conduct an audit of all 4 eligible entities that receive block grants under this section.

(g) MATCH REQUIREMENT.—An eligible entity that receives a grant under this section shall provide a non-Federal match in an amount equal to not less than—

(1) 15 percent of the grant during the first year;

(2) 25 percent of the grant during the first renewal period;

(3) 40 percent of the grant during the second renewal period; and

(4) 50 percent of the grant during the third renewal period.

(h) NO LIMITATION ON SECTION 204 GRANTS.—An entity that applies for a grant under section 204 is not prohibited from also applying for a grant under this section.

(i) AUTHORIZATION OF APPROPRIATIONS.—There are authorized to be appropriated $8,000,000 to the Attorney General for each of the fiscal years 2012 through 2015 to carry out this section.

(j) GAO EVALUATION.—Not later than 30 months after the date of the enactment of this Act, the Comptroller General of the United States shall submit a report to Congress that contains—

(1) an evaluation of the impact of this section in aiding minor victims of sex trafficking in the jurisdiction of the entity receiving the grant; and

(2) recommendations, if any, regarding any legislative or administrative action the Comptroller General determines appropriate.

SEC. 14044c. ENHANCING STATE AND LOCAL EFFORTS TO COMBAT TRAFFICKING IN PERSONS.

(a) ESTABLISHMENT OF GRANT PROGRAM FOR LAW ENFORCEMENT.—

(1) IN GENERAL.—The Attorney General may make grants to States and local law enforcement agencies to establish, develop, expand, or strengthen programs—

(A) to investigate and prosecute acts of severe forms of trafficking in persons, and related offenses[, which involve United States citizens, or aliens admitted for permanent residence, and] that occur, in whole or in part, within the territorial jurisdiction of the United States;

(B) to train law enforcement personnel how to identify victims of severe forms of trafficking in persons and related offenses;

[(B)]*(C)* to investigate and prosecute persons who engage in the purchase of commercial sex acts;

[(C)]*(D)* to educate persons charged with, or convicted of, purchasing or attempting to purchase commercial sex acts *and prioritize the investigations and prosecutions of those cases involving minor victims;* and

[(D)](E) to educate and train law enforcement personnel in how to establish trust of persons subjected to trafficking and encourage cooperation with prosecution efforts.

(2) DEFINITION.—In this subsection, the term "related offenses" includes violations of tax laws, transacting in illegally derived proceeds, money laundering, racketeering, and other violations of criminal laws committed in connection with an act of sex trafficking or a severe form of trafficking in persons.

(b) MULTI-DISCIPLINARY APPROACH REQUIRED.—Grants under subsection (a) of this section may be made only for programs in which the State or local law enforcement agency works collaboratively with social service providers and relevant nongovernmental organizations, including organizations with experience in the delivery of services to persons who are the subject of trafficking in persons.

(c) LIMITATION ON FEDERAL SHARE.—The Federal share of a grant made under this section may not exceed 75 percent of the total costs of the projects described in the application submitted.

(d) NO LIMITATION ON SECTION 14044A Grant Applications.—An entity that applies for a grant under section 202 is not prohibited from also applying for a grant under this section.

[(d)] *(e)* AUTHORIZATION OF APPROPRIATIONS.—There are authorized to be appropriated to the Attorney General to carry out this section [$20,000,000 for each of the fiscal years 2008 through 2011] *$10,000,000 for each of the fiscal years 2012 through 2015.*

(f) GAO EVALUATION AND REPORT.—Not later than 30 months after the date of enactment of this Act, the Comptroller General of the United States shall conduct a study of and submit to Congress a report evaluating the impact of this section on—

(1) the ability of law enforcement personnel to identify victims of severe forms of trafficking in persons and investigate and prosecute cases against offenders, including offenders who engage in the purchasing of commercial sex acts with a minor; and

(2) recommendations, if any, regarding any legislative or administrative action the Comptroller General determines appropriate to improve the ability described in paragraph (1).

*   *   *   *   *   *   *

SEC. 14044e. DEFINITIONS.

In this part:

(1) SEVERE FORMS OF TRAFFICKING IN PERSONS.—The term "severe forms of trafficking in persons" has the meaning given the term in [section 7102(8)] *section 7102(9)* of Title 22.

(2) SEX TRAFFICKING.—The term "sex trafficking" has the meaning given the term in [section 7102(9)] *section 7102(10)* of Title 22.

*   *   *   *   *   *   *

(3) COMMERCIAL SEX ACT.—The term "commercial sex act" has the meaning given the term in [section 7102(3)] *section 7102(4)* of Title 22.

SEC. 14044f. GRANTS FOR LAW ENFORCEMENT TRAINING PROGRAMS.

(a) DEFINITIONS.—In this section:

(1) ACT OF TRAFFICKING.—The term "act of trafficking" means an act or practice described in [paragraph (8)] paragraph (9) of section 7102 of Title 22.

(2) ELIGIBLE ENTITY.—The term "eligible entity" means a State or a local government.

(3) STATE.—The term "State" means any State of the United States, the District of Columbia, the Commonwealth of Puerto Rico, Guam, the United States Virgin Islands, the Commonwealth of the Northern Mariana Islands, American Samoa, and any other territory or possession of the United States.

(4) VICTIM OF TRAFFICKING.—The term "victim of trafficking" means a person subjected to an act of trafficking.

○